February 1981

PENGUIN EDUCATION

THE WORLD OF GOODS

MARY DOUGLAS AND BARON ISHERWOOD

The World of Goods

TOWARDS AN ANTHROPOLOGY OF CONSUMPTION

PENGUIN BOOKS

Penguin Books Ltd, Harmondsworth, Middlesex, England
Penguin Books, 625 Madison Avenue, New York, New York 10022, U.S.A.
Penguin Books Australia Ltd, Ringwood, Victoria, Australia
Penguin Books Canada Ltd, 2801 John Street, Markham, Ontario, Canada L3R 1B4
Penguin Books (N.Z.) Ltd, 182–190 Wairau Road, Auckland 10, New Zealand

—

First published in the United States of America by Basic Books, Inc., 1978
First published in Great Britain by Allen Lane 1979
Published in Penguin Education 1980

—

—

Made and printed in Great Britain by
Richard Clay (The Chaucer Press) Ltd., Bungay, Suffolk
Set in Times Roman

CONTENTS

ACKNOWLEDGMENTS

Work on this book would have gone on indefinitely, piecemeal and desultory, were it not for the invitation in 1971 from the University of Essex to give six lectures on a topic of cross-disciplinary interest, an invitation which started from a generous initiative of Penguin Books, hence the title "The Penguin Lectures." My first thanks are due, therefore, to the vice-chancellor of Essex University, Albert Sloman, and to the Faculties Board for the invitation and also for exceptional consideration, trustfulness, and patience. It was considerate of the Faculties Board to let me choose my topic, trustful to agree to one I had not yet started to study, and patient to wait for the study to be sufficiently advanced; then a double dose of patience for listening to lectures still patently not ready for publishing abroad, even by the summer of 1975. I recall the special kindness of P. D. A. Walker, the senior administrative officer, and of Stanley Cohen, then chairman of the sociology department, thanks to whom I was able to meet members of many different departments in Essex. I particularly thank Anthony King, Michael Bloxham, Ronald Atkin, Leonore Davidoff, Oliver Hart, and Alan Gelb for interesting discussions.

Originally, and a long time ago, my husband urged me to try a bridging task between economics and anthropology. The married state is a well-known forum for contesting different principles for the allocation of resources. The argument drove him to seek support in economic theory. But a science that claims to interpret demand fails every time it explains consumer behavior as irrational. If economic theory was a broken reed for domestic budgeting, its teachings at the level of the national budget could well be unsound. He long ago foretold that economists would be forced to repair a method that tried to explain consumption in terms of monetary rewards and constraints. In the chink between intuition and theory he saw that anthropology might provide a solution and urged me to talk to economists.

But though it was a pleasure in itself to exchange civilities with such a sophisticated and courteous set of people, it was soon clear I would have to learn some economics. To apply for study leave was the next step, but first I had to decide what sort of project to work upon. Since the issues hinged on budgeting, I thought at first that either public finance or monetary theory would be the appropriate field. Eventually, thanks to advice from Charles Goodhart and Robin Matthews, I steered towards the theory of consumption. Since they both have remained unstinting in their time and good counsel, I am particularly grateful for their support. If I had guessed how very difficult that field of work was to prove, I wonder if I could have stayed with it but for their encouragement. Perhaps I was foolhardy not to heed the distinguished economist, who, when he heard the project, declared it impossible and one from which he would consistently seek to dissuade me.

Vicky Chick and Morris Perlman earned my gratitude by mustering a distinguished list of economists to meet anthropologists on common ground in a seminar on means of payment in 1971. Aaron Wildavsky contributed a talk on budgeting processes in poor countries. His stimulus and support leave me greatly in his debt, for he has always seen so clearly that the sociologically interesting and inaccessible aspect of a budget is the underlying structure of assumptions which only surfaces in the form of a formidably steady-looking array of budgetary heads. The Social Science Research Council awarded me funds for research on a typology of budgetary systems and for an econometrician to be my research assistant on a special topic, the social monitoring of consumption. I have to thank M. G. Smith, head of the department of anthropology in University College, for a year's leave of absence (1973–74), which enabled me to start this research.

Acknowledgments

In November 1974, I made a short visit to Northwestern University to learn about the new home economics from Marc Nerlove, and through his good offices met Theodore Schultz, Margaret Reid, J. Mincer, G. Stigler, and Gary Becker and benefited from their kind hospitality and criticism. This visit turned out to be essential to my research and I wish such an opportunity might occur for all others who take up a difficult or lonely project. The benefits will not show enough in what I have written. An outsider starts with prejudices and resistances to the standpoint of a new subject. Timidity, ignorance, fidelity to the original inspiration, all combine to make learning difficult. The warm welcome and kind expenditure of time and thought lavished on me in Chicago and Evanston could not but induce a more receptive state of mind.

Another meeting on economic anthropology leads me to mention yet more names. A seminar on consumption held in 1974 in University College London was supported strongly by Morris Perlman, Alan Budd, Philip Burnham, Michael Thompson, Angus Deaton, Terence Gorman, John Muellbauer, Farouk Husein, and Owen Nankivell. In London in 1973 I was also lucky to be able to attend Anil Markandya's lectures on consumption at UCL and Richard Layard's seminar on the economics of education at the London School of Economics and to talk to the late Sigmund Zienau about the project. Louis Moss, Anne Jackson, Richard Stone, and Michael Bacharach were also very helpful at early stages and Albert Hirschman and Hans Singer at a later stage. I am also grateful to postgraduate students who also criticized stages of the work, particularly to José Llobera. David Worsley and Frank Blackaby were also generous with their time and gave me free use of the facilities of the National Institute of Economic and Social Research.

With so many persons to acknowledge, it is clear that their encouragement and helpfulness does not involve them in any responsibility for the outcome in general and for the particular uses to which their ideas have been put. After this experience,

I could never join the anthropologists who profess to despise economic analysis. For me, an abiding sense of the practice of a highly disciplined band of scholars, deeply concerned about methodology, is the most awe-inspiring outcome of the whole exercise.

The title comes from Donna Richards to whom I outlined the theme. She said that as a soldier's wife, adapted to a thoroughly mobile way of life, she could easily understand that a consumer's choice of goods is part of an attempt to impose identity and sense on the environment. She drew on Henry James's phrase "The empire of things" to illustrate the point. All our things have fallen into neglect while I have been writing, floors unpolished, curtains falling off hooks. I am grateful to my family for their patience.

MARY DOUGLAS

My own acknowledgments and thanks go to those social anthropologists and economists who have, in the fairly brief time that I have worked on the boundaries of the subjects, been sympathetic enough to encourage my participation in a wider and more colorful world and realistic enough to inhibit some of my more simplistic interpretations. For my introduction to social anthropology and anthropologists I must thank Caroline White and Robert Wade; for help with the manipulation of data I am grateful to Mick Maclean and Alan Coverdale, and to Alan Jarman for helpful discussions on the economics of social intercourse. The presentation of these ideas to the University College London consumption seminar, to a Social Sciences Research Council-sponsored conference on consumer behavior, and to a meeting of the Royal Statistical Society (RSS), led to a number of changes, and I am grateful to the numerous participants for their valuable criticisms, in particular Michael Thompson, Alan

Acknowledgments

Budd, and John Muellbauer. Above all I thank Nuala Swords who has in large part shared my own involvement with the research as it progressed, who was able to offer fruitful alternative approaches to some problems from her knowledge of sociological material, and whose attitude of sheer disbelief at important stages of the work often turned out to be an appropriate corrective.

BARON ISHERWOOD

The World of Goods

PREFACE

There is obloquy for merchandising and guilt in ownership. A growing swell of protest against the consumer society sets the background to this book. Consumerism is castigated as greed, stupidity, and insensitivity to want. Every month a new book inveighs against overconsumption and its vulgar display. But what are we to do about it? If it is our moral responsibility to live more austerely, we are notably reluctant to do so. Even if we were to divest our own life of surplus fat, our appearance in the bathroom mirror might please us better, but our slimming would hardly correct the evils of society. We would like to know how they live, the style and life of those moralists. Perhaps they give their royalties to the poor. Perhaps they spend judiciously as connoisseur collectors of rare manuscripts and paintings, or other forms of prestigious consumption which yield a good return on investment. But if the whole world were to invest in antiques, unemployment would soar still higher. Overconsumption is more serious and more complicated than personal obesity, and moral indignation is not enough for understanding it.

At present in the professional literature on consumption, there is a tendency to suppose that people buy goods for two or three restricted purposes: material welfare, psychic welfare, and display. The first two are needs of the individual person: the need to be fed, clothed, and sheltered, and for peace of mind and recreation. The last is a blanket term that covers all the demands of society. These then tend crudely to be summed up as competitive display. Thorstein Veblen has much to answer for when we consider how widely his analysis of the leisure class is received and how influential has been his unqualified scorn of conspicuous consumption. To turn the discussion into more realistic channels, several changes need to be made.

First, the very idea of consumption itself has to be set back into the social process, not merely looked upon as a result or objective of work. Consumption has to be recognized as an integral part of the same social system that accounts for the drive to work, itself part of the social need to relate to other people, and to have mediating materials for relating to them. Mediating materials are food, drink, and hospitality of home to offer, flowers and clothes to signal shared rejoicing, or mourning dress to share sorrow. Goods, work, and consumption have been artificially abstracted out of the whole social scheme. The way the excision has been made damages the possibility of understanding these aspects of our life.

To restore the unity would seem to be a start. But the problem goes so deep that nothing less profound than a corrected version of economic rationality is needed. For too long a narrow idea of human reasoning has prevailed which only accepts simple induction and deduction as worthy of the name of thinking. But there is a prior and pervasive kind of reasoning that scans a scene and sizes it up, packing into one instant's survey a process of matching, classifying, and comparing. This is not to invoke a mysterious faculty of intuition or mental association. Metaphoric appreciation, as all the words we have used suggest, is a work of approximate measurement, scaling and comparison between like and unlike elements in a pattern. The first half of this book establishes why and how the economist's idea of rationality ought to incorporate this code-breaking, jigsaw puzzle—solving activity of the human mind. By giving due credit to metaphorical understanding, we can come to a more accurate idea of why consumers buy goods.

To name one more familiar grief with economic theorizing: the idea of the rational individual is an impossible abstraction from social life. It is clearly absurd to aggregate millions of individuals buying and using goods without reckoning with the transformations they affect by sharing consumption together.

Once we have sunk the individual back into his social obligations and set consumption back into the social process, goods emerge with a very positive contribution to rational life, especially at the point of metaphorical reasoning. This book assumes that the rational being must fail to behave rationally, unless there is some consistency and reliability in the world around him. To continue to think rationally, the individual needs an intelligible universe, and that intelligibility will need to have some visible markings. Abstract concepts are always hard to remember, unless they take on some physical appearance. In this book, goods are treated as more or less costly, more or less transitory markers of rational categories. Behaving as an economic agent means making rational choices. Goods assembled together in ownership make physical, visible statements about the hierarchy of values to which their chooser subscribes. Goods can be cherished or judged inappropriate, discarded, and replaced. Unless we appreciate how they are used to constitute an intelligible universe, we will never know how to resolve the contradictions of our economic life.

In the protracted dialogue about value that is embedded in consumption, goods in their assemblage present a set of meanings, more or less coherent, more or less intentional. They are read by those who know the code and scan them for information. The great novelists have never doubted just how far removed this function of creating meanings is from the uses of goods for welfare and display. Henry James's great sensitivity on this score is particularly helpful. There are three rooms, each furnished by a rich woman. Each is seen for the first time by a visitor who in an instant's survey reads off some very pertinent general characteristics of the rooms, as well as the occupant's life and personality, and place in society. Note the speed of the reading. Note the private meanings which come across, as well as the intended ones. The first room shows a "supreme general adjustment to opportunities and conditions." The lady who gathered it together is going to be faded out of the tale, so it is in key with the delicate, resigned mood of the story's intractable tangles that she has evidently expected little from the visitor, but has made her apartment into a "final nest." Strether, the American hero of *The Ambassadors,* visited Miss Gostrey's home in Paris:

... This idea however was luckily all before him again from the moment he crossed the threshold of the little entresol of the Quartier Marboeuf into which she had gathered, as she said, picking them up in a thousand flights and funny little passionate pounces, the makings of a final nest.

... Her compact and crowded little chambers, almost dusky, as they at first struck him, with accumulations, represented a supreme general adjustment to opportunities and conditions. Wherever he looked he saw an old ivory or an old brocade, and he scarce knew where to sit for fear of a misappliance. . . . wide as his glimpse had lately become of the empire of "things," what was before him still enlarged it; the lust of the eyes and the pride of life had indeed thus their temple. It was the innermost nook of the shrine—as brown as a pirate's cave. In the brownness were glints of gold; patches of purple were in the gloom; objects all that caught, through the muslin, with their high rarity, the light of the low windows. Nothing was clear about them but that they were precious, and they brushed his ignorance with their contempt as a flower, in a liberty taken with him, might have been whisked under his nose. . . .

The goods brushed his ignorance with their contempt. So he failed the full reading test. If he had been better informed, they would have told him more. As it was, many of the meanings escaped him. She was evidently much more a connoisseur, more informed than he was about history and art. But other messages came across very precisely when the same visitor called on Madame de Vionnet:

... She occupied, his hostess, in the Rue de Bellechasse, the first floor of an old house to which our visitors had had access from an old clean court. The court was large and open, full of revelations, for our friend, of the habit of privacy, the peace of intervals, the dignity of distances and approaches; the house, to his restless sense, was in the high homely style of an elder day, and the ancient Paris that he was always looking for—sometimes intensely felt, sometimes more acutely missed—was in the immemorial polish of the wide waxed staircase and in the fine *boiseries,* the medallions, mouldings, mirrors, great clear spaces, of the greyish-white salon into which he had been shown. He seemed at the very outset to see her in the midst of possessions not vulgarly numerous, but hereditary, cherished, charming. . . . he found himself making out, as a background of the occupant, some glory, some prosperity of the First Empire, some Napoleonic glamour, some dim lustre of the great legend; elements clinging still to all the consular chairs and mythological brasses and sphinxes' heads and faded surfaces of satin striped with alternate silk.

The place itself went further back—that he guessed, and how old Paris continued in a manner to echo there; but the post-revolutionary period, the world he vaguely thought of as the world of Châteaubriand, of Madame de Staël, even of the young Lamartine, had left its stamp of harps and urns and torches, a stamp impressed on sundry small objects, ornaments and relics. He had never before, to his knowledge, had present to him relics, of any special dignity, of a private order—little old miniatures, medallions, pictures, books; books in leather bindings, pinkish and greenish, with gilt garlands on the back, ranged, together with other promiscuous properties, under the glass of brass-mounted cabinets. His attention took them all tenderly into account. They were among the matters that marked Madame de Vionnet's apartment as something quite different from Miss Gostrey's little museum of bargains and from Chad's lovely home; he recognised it as founded much more on old accumulations that had possibly from time to time shrunken than on any contemporary method of acquisition or form of curiosity. Chad and Miss Gostrey had rummaged and purchased and picked up and exchanged, sifting, selecting, comparing; whereas the mistress of the scene before him, beautifully passive under the spell of transmission—transmission from her father's line, he quite made up his mind—had only received, accepted and been quiet. When she hadn't been quiet she had been moved at the most to some occult charity for some fallen fortune. There had been objects she or her predecessors might even conceivably have parted with under need, but Strether couldn't suspect them of having sold old pieces to get "better" ones. They would have felt no difference as to better or worse. He could but imagine their having felt—perhaps in emigration, in proscription, for his sketch was slight and confused—the pressure of want or the obligation of sacrifice.

The pressure of want—whatever might be the case with the other force—was, however, presumably not active now, for the tokens of a chastened ease still abounded after all, many marks of a taste whose discriminations might perhaps have been called eccentric. He guessed at intense little preferences and sharp little exclusions, a deep suspicion of the vulgar and a personal view of the right.

Here is a lady surrounded by proofs of good breeding. He has called on her to discover the nature of her hold on his friend's nephew, to report whether she is a good woman and what exactly is her social position. In spite of the clear markers of lineage and trained discrimination, he receives an ambiguous impression: there is something a trifle odd.

. . . The general result of this was something for which he had no name on the spot quite ready, but something he would have come nearest to naming in speaking of it as the air of supreme respectability, the consciousness, small, still, reserved, but none the less distinct and diffused, of private honour. The air of supreme respectability—that was a strange blank wall for his adventure to have brought him to break his nose against. It had in fact, as he was now aware, filled all the approaches, hovered in the court as he passed, hung on the staircase as he mounted, sounded in the grave rumble of the old bell, as little electric as possible, of which Chad, at the door, had pulled the ancient but neatly-kept tassel; it formed in short the clearest medium of its particular kind that he had ever breathed. He would have answered for it at the end of a quarter of an hour that some of the glass cases contained swords and epaulettes of ancient colonels and generals; medals and orders once pinned over hearts that had long since ceased to beat; snuff-boxes bestowed on ministers and envoys; copies of works presented, with inscriptions, by authors now classic. . . . The fire, under the low white marble, undraped and academic, had burnt down to the silver ashes of light wood; one of the windows, at a distance, stood open to the mildness and stillness, out of which, in the short pauses, came the faint sound, pleasant and homely, almost rustic, of a plash and a clatter of sabots from some coach-house on the other side of the court.

As the tale proceeds, it turns out she is under great pressure to avoid the least hint of vulgarity or careless living. Of this controlled avoidance and desperate need for respectability, the assembly of objects spoke to him on first entering the court. The climax of the novel is the moment when he stumbles upon the illicit love which all that care to seem respectable was meant to conceal.

The third example is from *The Bostonians*. The Southerner visits his cousin in Boston.

The young man, left alone, looked about the parlour—the two parlours which, in their prolonged adjacent narrowness, formed evidently one apartment. . . . It seemed to him he had never seen an interior that was so much of an interior as this queer corridor-shaped drawing room of his newfound kinswoman; he had never felt himself in the presence of so much organized privacy or of so many objects that spoke of habits and tastes. . . . He had always heard of Boston as a city of culture, and now there was culture in Miss Chancellor's tables and sofas, in the books that were everywhere, on little shelves like brackets (as if a book were a statuette), in the photographs and water colours that covered the walls.

He also concluded that he would never be tempted to make love to the owner of the parlor. But then, recall that he had such different tastes. His concept of material comfort was not "very definite; it consisted mainly of the vision of plenty of cigars and brandy and water and newspapers, and a cane-bottom armchair of the right inclination from which he could stretch his legs."

To try to know the meaning of every one of these objects in any of the three rooms would have been a silly enterprise. The meaning of each is in its relation to the whole. Not one of the three rooms is used for competitive display. Finality, respectability, and privacy sum up the three readings.

Henry James himself has commented on this mode of reasoning which is carried in every stroke and touch, and which cannot be identified out of context but has to be understood from the whole collected work. *The Figure in the Carpet* (1896) is like an essay in gestalt psychology. The young literary critic is eager to know the secret of a writer, Vereker, whom he greatly admires. All his life he is trying to discover whether, before his death, Vereker had revealed his secret, as he put it, "Vereker's secret, my dear man, the general intention of his books; the string the pearls were strung on, the buried treasure, the figure in the carpet." But his interlocutors reply in blank surprise; they know nothing of it. By the end of the story we realize that what Vereker had told him originally is the only answer. He had once asked the great man: ". . . Meanwhile, just to hasten that difficult birth, can't you give a fellow a clue?" And was told, "My whole lucid effort gives him a clue—every page and line and letter. The things are as concrete there as a bird in a cage, a bait on a hook, a piece of cheese in a mousetrap. It is stuck into every volume as your foot is stuck into your shoe. It governs every line, it chooses every word, it dots every i, it places every comma." The secret is the total pattern, and apart from that totalizing creative effort, no single peg or clue can hold the meaning without travestying it. This is both how James wrote about writing and how he read the meanings of possessions.

Taking this answer and adding it to the critical methods now available, we can capture the effects of swift scanning by means of structural analysis. As this occasion ranks above that, and below this other one, so the goods fit to be used in it must be graded in rank to be an appropriate physical match for the gradations in value. On these lines there could be a beginning of a communication approach to consumption.

The first six chapters of this book develop the argument that goods are part of a live information system. The last part of the book tries to make use of this improved perspective by suggesting a different approach to social policy. Poverty, for lack of a better idea about goods, is conventionally treated either as an objective want of possessions or as a subjective feeling of envy and deprivation. But some are evidently poor yet not evidently conscious of being deprived. A tribesman with as many flocks and herds as he wants does not feel poor. He may lack electricity and air transport, but what of it? In the universe that he knows, if he has access to all the needful information and can disseminate his own views, he is not poor. The rightful measure of poverty, on this argument, is not possessions, but social involvement. Before concentrating on whether the, poor have enough to eat, we should, so this argument goes, worry about their links to the modern society. If their links into information are weak, sooner or later they will become so cut off that they are denied access to food and warmth.

But we should be concerned long before that stage is reached. The first things to worry about are the lines of communication. A household's expenditures on other people give an idea of whether it is isolated or well involved. This book introduces a distinction between small-scale consumption patterns, where the links with the wider society are short, fragile, and unconnected, and large-scale consumption patterns, which mean that the household is spending heavily on information of one kind or another. We have devised a way of measuring social involvement by comparing consumption patterns. We expect this measure to reveal more about social inequality than measures of income distribution do now.

Throughout the discussion we have compared households in distant, exotic places, where there are few markets and little merchandise, with our own homes. The insights from anthropology seem to train a powerful telescope upon ourselves. The best result we could hope for from this exercise would be to strip away the materials in which social relations are constituted, and see the bare patterns of the relationships which they cover. Then we would find that, having understood better the springs of rational choice, and having credited goods with a more important place in rational behavior, the consumer society is not absolved from guilt. Each free individual is responsible for the exclusiveness of his own home, the allocation of his free time, and hospitality. The moralists who indignantly condemn overconsumption will eventually have to answer for whom they do not invite to their table, how they wish their daughters to marry, where their old friends are today with whom they started out in their youth. Goods are neutral, their uses are social; they can be used as fences or bridges.

PART ONE

Goods as an
Information System

Chapter 1

WHY PEOPLE
WANT GOODS

Silence in Utility Theory

It is extraordinary to discover that no one knows why people want goods. Demand theory is at the very center, even at the origin of economics as a discipline. Yet 200 years of thought on the subject has little to show on the question. It is important to know why demand is sometimes stable, sometimes careers along with inflating speed, and sometimes goes slack while people save rather than spend. But economists carefully shun the question of why people want goods. They even count it a virtue not to offer suggestions. In the past, too many illicit intrusions from psychology have damaged their theoretical apparatus. It has now been painstakingly cleansed. It can answer questions about consumers' responses to changes in prices and incomes, so long as the period is short term and so long as "tastes" can be treated as given, as the ultimate unexplainable factor of demand that is used to explain everything else. On this academically restricted basis the machine can grind powerfully and exceedingly fine. But when it comes to policy problems, the theoretical gears mesh badly with social reality. The cool consensus that economists display on questions of economic method dissolves into a heated wrangle when a major economic crisis appears.

If theoretical economists try not to know about what makes the consumer tick, there are others who will not let him alone. They inveigh against the destructive greed of the consumer society, environmentalists and moralists, and economists, too, when wearing their "applied" hat. The consumer himself may well feel puzzled. With barely a twinge of guilt when he catches himself reaching for more furnishings or food, he partly supports the formal economist's view that his behavior is based on rational choice. He does not usually believe that he himself is a mindless moron, an easy victim for the advertiser's wiles, though he admits that others may be. He would agree that once he decides to get something, he chooses between brands and takes price and income level into account, much as the textbooks say. But the economist's view leaves much unexplained. Often it is not so much a sense of having made a decision but of having been overtaken by events. The new thing—the better lawn mower or bigger freezer—has somehow become, of its own accord, a necessity. It exerts its own imperative to be acquired and threatens that the household, without it, will regress to the chaos of a more primitive era. Far from exercising a sovereign choice, the wretched consumer, as often as not, feels like the passive holder of a wallet whose contents are preempted by such strong forces that moral reproaches seem impertinent.

Any vacuum sucks in its own filling. In the absence of an explicit account, implicit ideas about human needs creep into economic analysis unseen. The two main assumptions use each other for support, yet the combination is still dubious. On the one hand is the hygienic or materialist theory; on the other, the envy theory of needs. According to the first our real needs, most basic and universal, are our physical needs, those we have in common with livestock. Probably to avoid a too grossly veter-

inary approach, a curious moral split appears under the surface
of most economists' thoughts on human needs; they do recognize two kinds of needs, spiritual and physical, but they accord
priority to the physical. They allow it the dignity of a necessity,
while they downgrade all the other demands to a class of artificial wants, false, luxurious, even immoral. Luc Boltanski
calls this bias "biological Manicheeism." [1] That famous heresy
divided the universe between evil, the low biological side of
man's nature, and good, the spiritual side. But the economists
who make the same split unofficially change the heretical signs,
so that the biological becomes the good and the spiritual is
unjustified.

The hygiene approach seems to promise an objective definition of poverty since it can generally show that the poor in any
country have worse morbidity rates than the rich. But the promise is illusory, for it cannot deliver a way of defining poverty
cross-culturally that is not counterintuitive. True, this tribe or
that is poor in material things, its housing has to be remade
every year, its children run naked, its food is deficient in nu-
trients, its death rate is high—but are these sufficient to capture
the notion of poverty? If the hygiene standard is used alone,
improved death rates over the last 200 years would imply that
there are no poor left in England. In fact, however, poverty
studies never risk going out of business even in rich, industrial
societies, but they do face an awkward problem of definition.
Material standards have been indubitably raised: "Obviously
even those at the very foot of society in contemporary Britain
enjoy a standard of living that is somewhat higher than that of
the poorest in Victorian society a hundred years ago and much
higher than in many underdeveloped countries." [2] "People
who in this country are reckoned—or who reckon themselves—
poor today are not necessarily so by the standards of twenty-
five years ago or by the standards of other countries." [3] What
other countries? The hygienic criterion suggests those which
are malaria-ridden and lack public sanitation. Many of the

countries that anthropologists study are poor on such material criteria—no wall-to-wall carpets, no air conditioning—but they do not regard themselves as poor. The Nuer of the Sudan in the 1930s would do no trade with the Arabs because the only things they had to sell were their herds of cattle, and the only things they could possibly want from trade were more cattle.[4] Since the materialist approach cannot stand by itself, the economist is led to buttress it with a relativist view that invokes an envy theory to supplement materialism. "Poverty is a relative concept. Saying who is in poverty is to make a relative statement rather like saying who is short or heavy."[5] To explain the discontent in that relative condition, they are led to impute to the objects of their study feelings of covetousness and envy. For example, Albert Hirschmann believes in a universal feeling of envy which can be suspended by what he calls the "tunnel effect" at the beginning of a process of economic development.

"The tunnel effect operates because advances of others supply information about a more benign external environment; receipt of this information produces gratification; and this gratification overcomes, or at least suspends, envy. Though long noted as the most uninviting of the seven deadly sins because, unlike gluttony, pride, etc., it does not provide any initial fun to its practitioners, envy is nevertheless a powerful human emotion. This is attested to by the writings of anthropologists, sociologists, and economists, who all have proclaimed, in general quite independently of one another, that if you advance in income or status while I remain where I was, I will actually feel worse off than before because my relative position has declined."[6]

This is a very weak argument, however.

Anthropologists have written tomes on the subject of envy. Their fieldwork has forced it on their attention. Whatever they write about, whether about gifts, about witchcraft, demons, zombies, ancestors, or parish pump politics, their frequent point of reference is fear of envy, individual envy-deflecting techniques, and community envy-controlling edicts. If economists think that the demand for goods is influenced by envy, then anthropology is one place to turn for understanding it.[7] As we shall see, different types of social organization can be distinguished according to the envy-controlling techniques they deploy. The psychological state, unqualified by institutional differences, cannot do service for a subjective definition of poverty. Anyone can be envious, rich, or poor. But if we reject envy and keep materialism we are left with a mild wonder about the irrational human wish for fine carpets and new kitchens, much as one might question why dogs should want jeweled collars as well as food and exercise.

Fortunately a shift in emphasis is in the air. Titmuss wrote ". . . we have sought too diligently to find the causes of poverty among the poor and not in ourselves. . . . our frame of reference in the past has been too narrow. Thought, research, and action have been focused too heavily on the poor; poverty engineering has thus been abstracted from society." [8]

Self-criticism of Economists

There is no justification in traditional utility theory for assuming anything about physical or spiritual needs, still less about envy. The theory merely assumes the individual to be acting rationally, in that his choices are consistent with each other and stable over the short time that is relevant. It says that his tastes should be taken as given, that he responds to a fall in prices by readiness to buy a larger quantity and to a rise by buying less, and that he responds in consistent fashion to changes in his income. As he gets more of a particular good his desire for additional units of it weakens. For the anthropologist this minimum watertight rationality leaves the individual impossibly isolated. His rational objectives are tidied out of sight and trivialized under the term "tastes." It is hard to know where to begin to think about his social problems. But no rebuke that the anthropologist can deliver will be as severe as the self-criticism of the economists themselves on this very score.

Economists are their own harshest critics when it comes to the limitations of consumption theory, but naturally the strongest criticism comes from those who have some improvement to propose. Accordingly, Kelvin Lancaster said in a well-turned passage:

The theory of consumer behaviour in deterministic situations as set out by, say, Debreu (1959, 1960) or Uzama (1960) is a thing of great aesthetic beauty, a jewel set in a glass case. The product of a long process of refinement from the nineteenth century Utility theorists through Slutsky and Hicks-Allen to the economists of the last twenty-five years, it has been shorn of all irrelevant postulates so that it now stands as an example of how to extract the minimum of results from the minimum of assumptions.[9]

The criticisms are old, widespread, and still fashionable. "Hardly more than a collection of isolated, arbitrary definitions," Leontieff said, describing the theory of consumer behavior.[10] "One may wonder why such a theory has survived as a fundamental part of standard economics," said Michael and Becker. The defense usually falls back on the plea that demand theory, for all its weaknesses, still provides the most powerful method of analyzing choice. Indeed, it is probably true that there is no field of choice in which it cannot be used. But Michael and Becker will have none of this:

To whatever extent income and prices do not explain observed behaviour the explanation rests with variations in tastes, since they are the portmanteau in the demand curve. . . . For economists to rest a large part of their theory of choice on differences in tastes is disturbing, since they admittedly have no useful theory of the formation of tastes, nor can they rely on a well-developed theory of tastes from any other discipline in the social sciences, since none exists. Of course, by incorporating an intuitively appealing explanation in each case economists usually interpret these observations in reasonable ways. The important point, however, is that the received theory of choice itself is of modest use in that undertaking.[11]

To the inquiring anthropologist, the economists certainly seem to be unsatisfied consumers of their own product, and very self-critical of their own narrowness.

The early masters of economic theory were, in fact, intensely interested in the general determinants of economic progress and the broad conditions of wealth or poverty. The title *An Enquiry into the Nature and Causes of the Wealth of Nations* could not have been chosen by one who thought that the price mechanism in a short-run commodity market was the essence of economics. Adam Smith reached down to the fundamental factors that spell riches or poverty for a particular nation.[12]

That economics is still supposed to be reaching down into those factors, but has tied its own hands, is E. J. Mishan's plaint. Because of admitted ignorance about real conditions of existence, the economists, he says, have busily ferreted

out of welfare analysis all those tacit assumptions that appear to say something about the economic universe. But this purging of tacit empiricism has gone too far. Any generalisation but the most trivial is sure to collapse when all bounds to technical and behaviour possibilities are removed—when allowance is made for any and every imaginable situation. . . . What the subject badly needs is a strong infusion of empiricism to end its unchecked wanderings in the empyrean and to bring it down to earth feet first.[13]

If it were even agreed whether consumption was an end in itself or a means to an end, that would be a starting point. But sometimes consumption is treated as if it were a cost in keeping up the supply of healthy labor to the market, as if the consumer were a glorified carthorse to be fed, watered, and kept fit. Kuznets is not happy with this view; he remarks that over the long historical period of modern economic growth the

rise in food supply and improved health conditions should . . . have made for a better quality of the body of workers. But if the additional food, health and recreation outlays are treated as so many economic costs (rather than as final consumption), the implication would be that living is for work; and the distinction between final consumption, or product, and intermediate consumption, or costs, so basic in the ideological framework of modern society as well as in economic analysis and measurement, would be obliterated.[14]

On the other hand the more traditional view, treating consumption as the end or objective of all work [15] is equally objectionable. It demeans labor and disallows its right to be taken as an end in itself, always treating work as an input into something else.

As Frank Knight put it so wisely:

When we consider that productive activity takes up the larger part of the waking lives of the great mass of mankind, it is surely not to be assumed without investigation or inquiry that production is a means only, a necessary evil, a sacrifice made for the sake of some good entirely outside the production process. We are impelled to look for ends in the economic process itself, and to give thoughtful consideration to the possibilities of participation in economic activity as a sphere of self-expression and creative achievement.[16]

But Knight knew that he was working in a humane tradition. As Jevons insisted: "Economics does not rest upon the laws of human enjoyment; if these laws are developed by no other sciences they must be developed by economists." [17] And what about the challenge to Bentham's own account of utility? "By utility is meant that property in any object whereby it tends to produce benefit, advance, pleasure, good or happiness . . . or . . . to prevent the happening of mischief, pain, evil or unhappiness." [18] No one argues that human enjoyment should be separated off from work, but something in the construction of utility theory often makes it seem so.

Is there any reason why consumption should be found at the end or the beginning of a one-way avenue? Piero Sraffa identifies the tendency to focus on costs of production and outputs with the advent of the marginal method and deplores the loss of the earlier view of the economy as a seamless garment. His own *Production of Commodities by Means of Commodities* [19] is an attempt to restore something akin to "the original picture of the system of production and consumption as a circular process," . . . which "stands in striking contrast to the view presented by modern theory, of a one-way avenue that leads from 'Factors of Production' to 'Consumption Goods'." [20] His investigation "is concerned exclusively with such properties of an economic system as do not depend on changes in the scale of production or in the proportions of 'factors.' "

This standpoint, which is that of the old classical economists from Adam Smith to Ricardo, has been submerged and forgotten since the advent of the "marginal" method. The reason is obvious. The calculation of marginal differences requires attention to be focused on change, for without change either in the scale of an industry or in the proportions of the factors of production, "there can be neither marginal product nor marginal cost. In a system in which, day after day, production continued unchanged in those respects, the marginal product of a factor (or alternatively the marginal cost of a product) would not be merely hard to find—it just would not be there to be found." [21] The work that follows these prefatory remarks ought to be of great value to anthropology because of our tradition of working in the "ethnographic present." This is a special tense that aims to concentrate past, present, and future into a continuous present. Perhaps not always used honestly, the ethnographic present has more merit than a reconstructed and misconstrued time dimension. It synthesizes into one temporal point the events of many periods, the value of the synthesis lying in the strength of the analysis of the perceived present. Whatever is important about the past is assumed to be making itself known and felt here and now. Current ideas about the future likewise draw present judgments down certain paths and block off others. It assumes a two-way perspective in which the individual treats his past selectively as a source of validating myths and the future as the locus of dreams. The tense refers to a two-way filter being used in the present to sort out from the myths and dreams some sets that plausibly interlock as guides to action.

The ethnographic present assumes an unchanging economic system. Given the short time in which he has to do his research, the main problem to which a functional anthropologist of the 1950s and 1960s addressed himself was the understanding of an economy found in the here and now, a snapshot view, so implicitly deemed to be unchanging. The economic analysis explained how resources are channeled to the political and religious systems and the religious and political analyses explained how the economic system is sustained and credibly clothed in the raiment of distributive justice. Sraffa's book is too specialized and idiosyncratic to be directly useful to the anthropologist seeking to join issue with economists, but it is encouraging to realize that we have been speaking good prose without knowing it; we have been analyzing a circular process, so much so that the ethnographic picture could often be called production of ancestors by means of ancestors or production of cattle by means of cattle.

This is admittedly only a small qualification, not much to boast of, for entering a debate about the consumer society. One source of encouragement is that no one else seems to have much idea of why people want goods. When it comes to the other side of the same question, the reasons for not spending, there are also some intriguing misconceptions to straighten out.

Chapter 2

WHY THEY SAVE

According to Keynes

Saving is investment. It is also consumption postponed. As the level of future income depends on the amount of saving, the decision to consume now or to consume in the future is important in macroeconomics. In a famous passage Keynes declared that a psychological rule causes men to be disposed to increase their consumption as their income increases, but not by as much as by the increase in income.

These considerations will lead, as a rule, to a greater proportion of income being saved as real income rises. . . . We take it as a fundamental psychological rule of any modern community that, when its real income is increased it will not increase its consumption by an absolute equal amount, so that a greater amount must be saved.[1]

This "rule" relates the propensity to consume to a capacity to be satisfied at a particular level of real income. It relates it thereby implicitly to a capacity of goods themselves to satisfy "real" wants. It might be assumed, therefore, that in the past century, when real income has increased steadily and impressively, the proportion saved out of income should have increased accordingly. But the long historical rise in real income has not been accompanied by a proportionate rise in savings. To the anthropologist it would be very surprising if it had. That savings should have increased in a regular fashion over a long period just because real income was increasing is difficult to credit. If we start with the assumption that saving is socially determined and that it would therefore be most unlikely to be affected by real income, it seems equally reasonable to posit a culture in which everyone is expected to die insolvent, or to balance exactly their expenditures and income over a year, or some other socially agreed rule. It does not seem at all surprising that the simple Keynesian principle does not hold. The alternative principle attributed to Kuznets of "a long-run secular dissipation" of the tendency to save a higher proportion with rising real per capita income [2] seems more plausible because it could link spending with social conditions conducive to a rising real income.

Being a slow spender is not always and everywhere held to be better than being openhanded. Each culture cuts its slices of moral reality in a different way and metes approval and disapproval to counterpoised virtues and vices according to the local views. But it is interesting to observe the very different values that different societies set on the ratio of consumption to income. Spending only a small proportion of income may in one place and time be called thrifty, wise, and provident; in another it may be held to be miserly, mean, and wrong. Conversely, a high ratio of consumption may be approved as generous, magnificent, and good in one culture, while in another the selfsame behavior may be called spendthrift, feckless, and bad. Evidently, the social context that generates the appropriate judgment must be worth examining.

Irving Fisher used the word "impatience" to refer to any economy that showed a tendency to run down resources.[3] That tendency is still discussed and disapproved in current thinking about the environment. In quite another context the idea of impatience attracts disapproval when it is used to describe the low level of investment in some underdeveloped countries. Here impatience means that the demands of the present are too urgent to be denied. A strong time preference is often treated as if it implied a strong leisure preference—as if the longing to rest and sleep or the longing to eat, drink, and make merry has priority over the need to provide for the future. To speak of the poor as having a strong subjective time preference or a high rate of time—cost discounting can only be supported in circular fashion by the fact that the poor sections of the population are defined as those with the least assets and who may for that very reason be said to live in the present and even to have a characteristic short-term structuring of time.[4]

The judgments thrifty, mean, spendthrift, feckless, magnificent, generous, if they are strongly delivered by the rest of the social environment, can effectively set a ceiling and floor to individual expenditure. Such judgments are the source of the very cultural norms that anthropologists study. In what follows I will try to relate these social judgments on spending to three distinctive bodies of work: first, Max Weber's account of *The Rise of the Protestant Ethic and the Spirit of Capitalism*,[5] and to the theories of consumption and saving of the two economists James Duesenberry and Milton Friedman.

According to Weber

Weber analyzed the historical shift from conspicuous Renaissance splendor to sixteenth and seventeenth century economic calculation, as a simultaneous change at three levels, socioeconomic, doctrinal, and moral. He contrasted an earlier Catholic mode that disapproved of private accumulation with a later Protestant mode that approved of it. In economic matters the first view discouraged individual calculation and the second encouraged it. In doctrinal matters the first pointed to blessings in the hereafter as the reward of good behavior, while the second regarded blessings in this world as a sign of behavior being justified; in ethics, religion and the religious calling were specialized in Catholicism, set apart from and superior to gaining a living in the lay condition, but in Protestantism the distinction disappeared, and all ways of gaining a livelihood were treated as a religious calling in itself. This three-tier approach is exactly the right one for the anthropologist to follow. It suggests a seamless garment, the economy, with its adjusted political institutions, its adjusted religious doctrines, and its adjusted ethics, each supporting the other. Pick up the thread anywhere and follow it around—it will lead back to the same place. This way will not allow us to make a sharp and arbitrary break between parts of the economic process. There will be two advantages. For one, the anthropologists' synthesizing bias may usefully supplant the economists' analytic one. For another, the individual, seen both as a consumer and as a producer, will turn out to behave rationally.

Max Weber only developed the analysis of two economic-doctrinal types, but he suggests two more, making a total of four. We quote:

It is one of the fundamental characteristics of an individualistic capitalist economy that it is rationalised on the basis of rigorous calculation, directed with foresight and caution towards the economic success which is sought in sharp contrast to the hand to mouth existence of the peasant, and to the privileged traditionalism of the guild craftsman and the adventurer's capitalism, oriented to the exploitation of political opportunities and irrational speculation.[6]

So here we have four types:

1. The traditional economy
2. The hand-to-mouth existence of the peasant
3. Adventurer's capitalism
4. Individual capitalist economy

He says nothing more in this essay on the hand-to-mouth existence of the peasant or on adventurer's capitalism. There was a case for treating both as peripheral to the main march of

TABLE 2-1

Case 1 – Economic Traditional

Example	Goal	Rationalization	Means	Private Consumption	Private Savings
Thirteenth Century Guild craftsman	To reinforce privilege of traditional classes	Otherworldly salvation; the concept of a sufficiency for life	Tight regulation of economic life; control of usury; traditional fixed prices and hours of work; moral control of business conduct; forced redistribution	Fixed standard, including leisure; low level of normal consumption	Corporate savings enormous; private savings kept low or limited to fringes of political society

Case 2 – Individual Capitalist Economy

Example	Goal	Rationalization	Means	Private Consumption	Private Savings
Benjamin Franklin's printing press and other small businesses; pietist peasants of Westphalia	Economic success of individual	A calling in this world; worldly asceticism; the civic benefits of individual prosperity	The rational calculation applied to individual profit	Kept low by asceticism	Individual savings in private business high

history and ignoring them in this analysis. The spread of these four types through different periods and places is a crucial part of his argument against seeking economic and institutional determinants and his reason for turning to the spirit of the age to explain the revolution in behavior in Europe from the sixteenth century until today. In practice all his interest is concentrated on the other two, and his argument deals with the shift from what he depicts as the traditional to the individualist capitalist economy, summarized in table 2–1.

He gives so much illustration from small craftsmen and small businesses in both cases that the movement he is seeking to identify would seem to derive from small craftsmen, originally needing little capital equipment or work force, and developing into expanding private businesses, a revolution in economic organization responding to the strong pressure for the division of labor at the time of European expansion. The approach that the anthropologist would prefer to explore, before turning to the spirit of the age, would pay much more attention to the social and economic relations of individuals in the two cases, and to the way that their changed social environment would be likely to affect their perception of moral issues.

An anthropological approach to saving will need to pick up the neglected peripheral cases and to develop a description of possible social environments which will include them along with the mainstream. Concerning the peasants and their hand-to-mouth existence, we can distinguish many interesting variants according to their incentives to produce,[7] the strength of their dependence on outside markets, and the strength of the resulting boundary separating their world from the rest of society.[8] As to the adventurous capitalists gambling in political speculation, we shall be equally interested in them. They are likely to live wildly beyond their incomes, but they are not irrationally ready to give everything away at ecclesiastical behest. It would be naive to mark them up as otherworldly because of their lavish legacies to the Church.

It is hard to disentangle Weber's three-layer analysis from the historical particularities in which the subject was set, and so it has never given rise to a general sociological theory of saving. Before I start to sink it into a larger scheme, let me bracket away or clarify two parts of Weber's analysis that are misleading. One is the recourse to the spirit of the age, the spirit of capitalism, as the independent explanatory variable. The elaborated footnotes to the book reiterate the independent role of this spirit in his analysis, but I choose to ignore them. This is because what may have been all right for the master has become too facile for the disciples. How the spirit of the age is generated is precisely what we want to discover. To be allowed to assume that the spirit (or the "culture" in the case of anthropologists) has independent explanatory power is worse than mistaken—it shows a deplorable want of curiosity and allows the sociologist to bring his investigation to a halt the moment it seems to support his favorite thesis. Therefore we shall assume, following the stronger trend of Weber's thought, that the doctrinal and ethical interpretations that characterize an age and its spirit are only part of the thing to be analyzed and are not independent agencies.

The second caveat relates to the alleged otherworldliness of Catholic doctrines in contrast with the this-worldliness of Protestantism. This follows and is included in the warning in the last paragraph. Never should it be possible for anyone to explain any socioeconomic behavior by saying "Ah, they behave like this, etc., etc., because of their Catholic, Hindu, Confucian, etc., doctrines." The doctrines cannot explain anything without providing some adequate reason for people's allegiance to them. Neither doctrines nor allegiances are fixed. The sociologist will have to think of reasons why a pie-in-the-sky doctrine of afterlife compensation for the dissipation of a worldly fortune becomes acceptable. How it credibly becomes good sense to give away everything to the poor is a problem within the circular analysis in which the anthropologist has specialized. Only if he can think of convincing nondoctrinal reasons for adherence to a given doctrine will he be on the way to explaining how particular doctrines are generated. As it happens, the Catholic case is not unique. Many peoples in different cultures believe in heavenly rewards for altruism. There may be nothing especially otherworldly (quite the reverse) about the general tone of a culture that promises a glorious afterlife for deeds it cannot otherwise reward, though the people who fall for the promise are behaving in an otherworldly way, all right. The Vikings had their Valhalla; the Eskimos believe in a specially comfortable, posthumous nook for the man or woman who saves food for the starving camp by walking out into the blizzard; North American Indians had happy hunting grounds for great warriors; and African ancestor cults lay down the way to behave if you want one day to grow into an ancestor yourself. There is a military nexus, a political nexus, or a straight cash nexus. When otherworldliness appears, one sector is usually bribing another sector of society, and our interest should focus on the balance of power between the sectors. In the case of pre-Reformation Europe, when the clergy were prevailing on the landlords, knights, and merchants to part with lands, cash, and booty, the clergy themselves were behaving in a notably this-worldly fashion as far as their own interests were concerned. The use of the valuable ethnographic present forces us to give full weight to the here and now in interpreting theories about life beyond the grave. In an environment in which strong groups are strongly competing, brokers and mercenaries inevitably will emerge, ready to work for either side for an appropriate commission. To sign a magnificent deed of gift to one group or another may be a painless piece of rational economic and political sense, especially if the gift is not to be transferred in the donor's lifetime.

A splendid account of adventures and the general environment which Weber was describing as pre-Reformation and traditional Catholic comes in Boutruche's study of the Hundred

Years War in the Bordeaux region.[9] Here it is evident that all four economic types are struggling together, as Weber freely recognized. Clearly the contest of powerful groups creates a certain environment, with immense prizes at stake and uncertain rules as the war is waged back and forth across the territory. But we would insist that the wild extravagance of the princely and ducal courts was undoubtedly less due to a lively faith in the world to come than to a rational and calculating overconsumption, an investment in conspicuous loyalty that might, with luck, pay handsome dividends. During this war between the English and the French kings, in which the great lords were either high nobility or high clergy (and often both), land was the stake they fought for at every level. Royalty, great nobles, and lesser nobles, each a link in the chain of dependence, could only live as befitted their class by the revenues from land.

In the thirteenth century the English king, trying to secure his Bordeaux territory, reinforced the loyalty of local lords by his own presence in times of crisis, or by sending his heir or another member of his family. After Edward I, the Black Prince came once; then came the Dukes of Lancaster, Clarence, Derby, Talbot. The administration was a mixture of ancient feudalism and modern techniques, a combination distinctly ineffectual and giving great scope to arbitrary and unforeseen ad hoc powers. In the weak and confused administrative system personal links were all-important. On the English side, movement between the two countries was frequent; intermarriage was frequent also. The Bordelais saw no conflict of conscience in following their feudal lord when he fought the king of France, and they saw much economic advantage in the link with England. The troops of the king of France were resisted not only by the English soldiers, but also by all the vineyard owners and merchants who saw the fleur-de-lys threatening their trading outlets. But some among the nobles had no such clear-cut choice. Each leader scanned his host, calculated who among his vassals was weakening in loyalty so as to renew attempts to hold them, and would equally scan the followers on the other side whom he might hope to win over.[10] With veiled threats and blandishments he would warn his own men against the evil machinations of the enemy. Between the main ranks of adversaries stood a confused crisscross of lords who sniffed the wind, weighed the risks of a change of allegiance, and passed from one camp into the other, trafficking in loyalty. Raymond IV, Vicomte de Fronsac, owner of a river fortress, changed sides five times from 1336–1349. The Budes, border lords, decided eventually after three switches to stay with the French when the Duke of Anjou recaptured their region. In 1377 the Durfort rallied permanently to the English after many a previous turnabout. In such an environment, when perjured oaths were as much a career as a necessity, the kings of England and France would confiscate the estates of nobles and dance them before the eyes of the hesitant. They were surrounded with nobles complaining of having been robbed of their heritage by the enemy and demanding compensation or a fief while waiting for deliverance of their family lands. Listing their devoted services, they would hint that the enemy would be more generous. Feudal dependence became a chain of blackmail, the kings openly handing out feudal rights as the price of conscience.

When it comes to describing the dissipation of their fortunes by lavish good living at court, Boutruche excuses their overspending by saying that absence from their lands made them unrealistic. But the anthropological analysis shows that in those competitive times, a lord who did not make a good show of himself and his following risked oblivion, and oblivion would surely end in his estates being given to a more pressing claimant on the king's good will. This applied to the rival kings as much as to their lords. Boutruche is also very kindly about the bequests they made, arguing that the same lack of realism that made them spend more than their income flowed over into their will-making, proving that they just didn't know the exact amount of their fortunes, slashed by mortgages and debts. But it could equally be argued that it was not irrational or unrealistic to make generous legacies and leave to their executors the task of carrying them out.

Interestingly, though everything that has been said about the lavish expenditure of nobles applies also to the clergy, the latter were constrained in one respect. Noble fortunes were mutilated by last wills and testaments, but the lords of the Church were not allowed to sell or to mortgage land—an example of how a strong corporate group protects group property.

The clergy win on every score. For the great lords compete with one another for the credit of posthumous generosity to the Church. They must have known that they were destroying the future of their family, and their wills suggest that the bequest motive is a case for the ethnographic present, less a concern for posterity than for present satisfaction. They were able to boast of the thousands of masses they were offering, the monuments, chapels, doors, and windows they were donating, the Crusades or pilgrimages they were contributing to. To convince an anthropologist that they acted from pure otherworldly motives it would be necessary to make the unlikely claim that the Church had no political power worth enlisting. Their heirs sold land to fulfill their promises, and the land was bought by the professionals who were the current teachers on piety and promise-keeping: the Franciscans, Augustinians, Carmelites, and Dominicans.[11] "In the twilight of the Middle Ages the Church remained the dominant capitalist power of the Bordelais," taking the long view, as a well-established group can do, and behaving as to economic policy in a very this-worldly way. At that time individuals were not saving, but corporate groups were; the Protestant ethic takes over from pre-Reformation otherworldliness when the balance of power is reversed and when corporate groups lose out to the claims of individuals.

The Group Environment

An anthropological account of social environments and their effect on saving can well start by counterpoising the individual to the group. Our most distinctive model of the group is the corporate lineage.[12] Corporations, if they have a defined membership, take common decisions, administer common property (even if it is only a reputation attached to a name) and tend to behave as if they were to live forever. Individuals who belong in such units, and who act on their behalf, are under pressure to take the long view.

Certain institutions in our society operate in full recognition of the difference between long-term and short-term changes. They directly "produce" much of the former. . . . Even an individual, short as the span of his life may be, . . . considers the long-term trend of his active life, prepares for it and allows for it; . . . a similar argument applies with greater force regarding individuals in their capacity as members of business enterprises or of other institutional units; . . . in theory, and often in actual practice, these non-family institutions act as if endowed with eternal life. Their time-horizon, therefore, can be, and often is, much wider than that of individuals acting as members of family units; they are even more cognisant of the difference between the long and the short run.[13]

The group can claim to represent not only the longest view, but also the public interest. This claim protects it from envy. The group can therefore levy a tax on its members, distrain their goods, and do what it likes so long as the claim to the long view and the public interest is plausible. If we were to place different societies along a hypothetical scale from weak towards strong, the stronger the group the greater its capacity to accumulate assets in its own name and the less the power of its constituent members to accumulate assets for themselves. A strong group has its own characteristic ways of controlling the envy that might spoil the relations of its members and so threaten its permanence.

The group imposes group values and so prevents deviant individual spending, defines what counts as too much conspicuous individual consumption, and proposes punishments. As part of the process of strengthening its hold on individual members, the group makes levies on their time and income. The effect is redistributive as between members and probably lowers the gross output of the group. The demand that the rich man give a feast ensures that all enjoy something of the accumulation, but it also tends to ensure that it is dissipated. As the group moves to greater strength in the defining of its boundaries, so rules for admission to the group and to the franchise of its privileges tighten. No one belongs who cannot be seen to qualify for membership, so capricious envy is controlled by clarity of definition. It sets a ceiling on individual accumulation by its approval for a certain standard of consumption and disapproval of excess. Either it requires uniformity of wealth or uses a theory of distributive justice which demonstrates that tolerable inequalities of wealth are related to the unequal load of group responsibility. "Chiefs are slaves," groans the African chief, owner of the biggest herds in the tribe, thereby claiming that his endless chores, administrative and legislative, are far more burdensome than any private wealth could possibly recompense. There are plenty of examples in the anthropology of exotic places, but these characteristics of how a strong group's effective time–cost discounting emerges is also nicely illustrated in the study of Ashton, a Yorkshire mining village to be described in chapter 8.

Its long-time perspective is an integral part of the group's entitlement to a superior moral status. Because its legal existence is eternal, it can make its demands in the name of unborn generations. It can use the bequest motive as a stick to belabor its stingy members. No individual acting on his or her own behalf can entertain dreams of such a long-term future. Only the group can develop a full-fledged otherworldly morality, for the group outlives its members. Thus, we conclude that the otherworldliness of a doctrinal bias is dependent on the strength of group and the need for altruistic sacrifices that is perceived by its representatives. Note how the group environment fulfills the conditions needed for Weber's traditional economy. But in spite of all the advantages that it can draw to itself, the group is fragile and by no means ubiquitous.

The Individualist Environment

A group's intended eternity is always at risk from depradations —from within or from more powerful rival corporations. Consequently, we must also turn to the very active branch of anthropology which has concentrated on individual transactions; particularly relevant is network analysis which is used to examine the structure of relationships in societies where groups are ephemeral or less important. In view of some economists' interest in envy as the mainspring of demand, it is worth asking how envy is controlled in the absence of group boundaries and group morality.

It is relatively easy to describe a social environment when one can set the individual against the backdrop of a group. But when it comes to thinking about a social environment that is initially defined by absence of groups and is characterized rather by the transactions of individuals with one another, sociologists have to make the same kind of theoretical effort that economists made when they first started to assess systematically the externalities of transactions. This environment which is created for individuals by their reciprocal interaction, we shall call "grid." (See figure 2–1.) At the top end the grid is strong. It consists of insulations between individuals which prevent free transaction. The rate of interaction might be lowered either by sheer physical isolation or by self-made rules. Sometimes the members of a restricted social class may conceive that there are

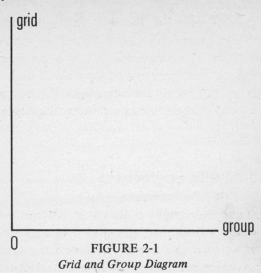

FIGURE 2-1
Grid and Group Diagram

only a few families into which they can possibly allow their offspring to marry; the various cross-classifications of birth, age, wealth, and actual standing may even result in a particular individual having no possible marriage partner or only one. Such insulations, which may take the form of classifications that account exhaustively for the condition of individuals while preventing them from freely transacting, we shall call "strong grid." Moving down the scale, as insulation weakens, individuals have more scope to deal with one another as they wish. The move away from the insulation of strong grid is not necessarily a move to disorganization and a lack of rule. To permit the maximum possible number of contracts fairly entered, their conditions known and their performance assessable, a new form of control emerges: the invisible control of fair-comparison rules. From the courts of chivalry to Marquis of Queensbury rules, or from the cattle market to the stock exchange, the effect of these rules is to regularize competition, to ensure a fair contest, and to hold the parties to a contract to their pledged word. This, which we shall call "weak grid," favors strong individualism. (Basil Bernstein worked out the whole of this analysis of classification for application to institutions of learning and we have derived our own use of it from his theory.) [14] To summarize an extensive ethnographic record, it can be said that in a scaled dimension from strong to weak grid, there is no need for envy to be put under definition or controlled where the insulations themselves separate people from one another. But as individualism becomes the recognized order of the day, the disruptive energies of envy may be a dangerous threat to safety of life and property, the more so because a free market in individual transactions always seems to result in an uneven distribution of influence and wealth, and an appropriate theory of distributive justice is needed to make it acceptable.

In weak-grid, weak-group societies, instead of group values being imposed on the individual, the latter's personal responsibility is crystallized in the triangle of honor, shame, and luck. The words are not always the same, of course, for we have taken the terms from our own civilization, exemplified in Mediterranean studies.[15] For other times and places there are closely equivalent ideas.[16] Instead of accepting their allotted station in a given scheme of things, as where grid is strong, each family is involved, for its very survival, in the effort for advantageous alliances—marital, defensive, or financial. It must be so; for the relations between individuals being governed by fiercely contested ranking, rather than by group values, there are no redistributive levies, no checks on spending or saving. According to the pattern of alliances made, there will also be a greater degree of inequality. There will be big fortunes and small, just as there are big battalions that tend to grow bigger and small ones whose supporters desert them. Inevitably personal honor will be connected with success in the struggle for alliance, and the penalty for failure will be shame. Instead of rules for admission to the group and its privileges, we find that theories of purity—purity of women, purity of ritual, purity of food—are invoked to supply tests of fitness for upward mobility and to create techniques of selective exclusion; a relation between pure living and success will be invoked and become part of the rules governing transactions.[17] Instead of caring about rules creating uniformity of wealth, the people will care greatly about rules governing the equality and fairness of the contest between individuals. This may be elaborated to become the principal envy-controlling instrument of such a social environment.

In this type of environment, a man who is judged a failure will also be judged wanting in the required moral and intellectual stamina to sustain the honor of his family, so he will merit the shame he endures. But so that the less fortunate—those who may claim plausibly that they have been both virtuous and clever, and yet have not received high rewards—do not bring the whole system into question, there must be another quality, usually another initial endowment, nothing to do with morality or cleverness, to justify the distribution of rewards. It was luck for our forefathers, the Norsemen, destiny in the case of the Greeks, the caprice of a spirit-sponsor in the Plains Indians society, predestination in modern Calvinism. When luck, shame, and honor have replaced the avenging ancestors as controlling ideas, we have moved away from a society that is regulated by reference to any hereafter to one explicitly concerned with this world. So we can return, fortified, to Weber's four types (see figure 2–2) and ask how individual thrift and savings will fare in each.

These are meant to represent four stable types of environment. The adventurer capitalists do not quite fit into the scheme we have drawn up if they are of the wildly extravagant type we have described for the Bordeaux nobles in the Hundred Years' War. But as soon as they could steady allegiances in a less agitated state, they could move into the kind of society near the zero point of bottom left. We have inserted, to complete Weber's picture, the great corporations of the Church at bottom right. At the top left are the peasants, as he referred to them. Their hand-to-mouth existence fits strong insulation, strong grid. We need say nothing here about rigid control by landlords or low returns for investment; these are part of the system which

peasants	traditional society
individualist capitalism adventurers	convents, monasteries and bishoprics

FIGURE 2-2
Weber's Four Types

strongly classifies them into the periphery of the main society, so that they can neither compete with one another nor unite against oppressors. They would save, but their low level of output makes it difficult.

The possibility for private individual accumulation is weakest for the right-hand side of the diagram where the individual store is constantly raided for group purposes. Weber's idea of the traditional economy, marked by restrictive practices and equalizing rules, and a rejection of individual accumulation, fits in here. The individual saves little, but the group accumulates wealth. Guildhalls and cathedrals get endowed and built. The otherworldly doctrine is one of the ways in which this pattern of behavior is made intelligible and acceptable. Strong individualism (weak grid) gives the greatest incentives to private accumulation. But the rules are hard to satisfy and though the rewards may be great, success is a risk, as Weber himself pointed out in calling the adventurer class speculative political gamblers. The individualist capitalist economy—exemplified for Weber by Benjamin Franklin, extolling the virtues of honesty, industry, and solvency which uphold the rules of interaction—is somewhere fairly low along the line of grid, possibly a little to the middle, if the common rules of commerce which are agreed upon attest to some strong group consensus.

This scheme of possible social environments, each with its particular effect on individual savings, allows the examples from Max Weber's study to be remapped, his weaknesses corrected, and his typology of sixteenth-century Europe sunk into a more universal paradigm that can take account of tribal or of modern times. One of the reasons why it is important to develop a grid and group analysis is that we can identify the trends in modern industrial society which are progressively releasing the individual from the close control of strong grid and the coercion of the bonded group. But instead of being released to freedom, the individual is then drawn into a very difficult social environment, the bottom left-hand corner of the diagram, where he must either compete or be despised as a deviant; and if he competes he must risk shame and seek honor, trust to luck, and create ever more uncertainty for all in his entourage, so that they too will come to value honor, avoid shame, and trust to luck. That environment is a very harsh one to endure, and for that reason, individuals either opt out of it by seeking to hedge off a commune of like-minded souls, or they are forced out of it by being forced into a position of minimum choice and maximum isolation.

Probably one of the most important reasons of all for understanding this analysis is that the wish to escape from grid and group control throws up small groups. Alternatively, it creates enormous disparities of wealth and power. The environment of strong individualism is not egalitarian in its distributive effects.

Emulation According to Duesenberry

It seems extraordinary, but it is an outcome of the way that traditional utility theory has been used, that the consuming unit acts as if its decisions to spend on this or that were made in isolation and independently from those of all other consumers. Advertisers and market researchers know about the social factors, class, age, and competitiveness. Sociologists and anthropologists know that consumption standards are socially determined. But before 1949 economists still found that a demand theory based on the isolated individual was adequate to explain consumption decisions as functions of prices and income alone. At least it was adequate for the two purposes it was designed to serve. It was useful for attacking the previous dominant position according to which prices were mainly determined by costs. It was also useful for predicting the behavior of quantities on prices in particular markets. For these limited purposes there was no need to pay special attention to the social factors determining consumption. This individualistic and atomized model of the consumer was at last formally attacked by Duesenberry.[18]

It seems astonishing that as late as 1949 the two assumptions he criticized were still firmly entrenched: (1) that every individual's consumption behavior is independent of all other individuals', and (2) that consumption decisions are reversible in time.

The reason for making an attack at that time was a shift in focus of interest. The effect of consumer behavior on prices was covered by existing theory. But the existing theory was not adequate to explain saving behavior. Keynes's fundamental psychological rule left plenty of scope for clarification. Duesenberry was the first economist for a very long time to seek a sociological instead of a psychological theory.

Here at least is an economist with sophisticated views about the social nature of human needs. He does not mean to be distracted by any false distinction between basic physical needs and social requirements for luxury and competition. As he says, goods are goods in virtue of being specialized for certain activities; generally, a culturally agreed scale ranks goods for any given purpose; and the only freedom from the cultural constraint which an individual enjoys when choosing consumption goods is the scope for varying the quality within the range of his income. But however much he professes to be unconcerned with moral and social judgments about the objects of expenditure, Duesenberry slips sometimes into disapproval of high value set on the acquisition of material things. If he consistently rejected any distinction between real and socially determined standards, he would have no criterion to justify the distinction he makes between useful and "completely useless goods" [19] and if he were really concerned to establish a universal basis for the comparison of consumption patterns, this confusion would matter. But as it is, he is concerned only to understand one culture in which high consumption standards enter into the competition for differentiated social status. He makes a neat comparison between the American consuming public and Cora Dubois's *People of Alor*,[20] both societies in which envy and competitive display spur the individual to ever higher standards of living.

Duesenberry challenges Keynes on the responsiveness of the ratio of consumption to changes in income. For the kind of society Duesenberry is describing, there is continual pressure on the consumer to spend more. As a start to considering the marginal propensity to consume, Duesenberry would separate the propensity to save from the absolute level of income, relating it to a more directly social factor, that is, the relative position of the consumer in the income distribution of his population. By inference, for him, a separate population is a subculture, since it exerts distinctive pressures to consume on its members. A person whose income is relatively high will have been able to satisfy all the requirements socially imposed upon him and so will have a residue for saving. One whose income is low will always be shelling out to meet those cultural demands and will never be able to save. Duesenberry's sociological theory has a few simple principles: the culturally mediated pressure to consume, the cultural boundary of a population, a universal principle of social emulation within a given culture, savings as feasible nonconsumption after the cultural pressures have been satisfied. One of the obvious limitations of his approach is that he treats savings as a residual category.

With this kit he is able to show why changes in real income over a long period have had little effect on the consumption ratio. We started out by remarking that even if Keynes's law holds good over a cross section of a modern economy, it fails in data supplied from time series. Duesenberry would argue that this is because continuous cultural change makes rising demands for increased consumption, a very acceptable and sympathetic argument to the anthropologist. In each period, as it were, we are dealing with a different culture with its own new standards of consumption. The tidiest example with which he proves his point is the comparison of blacks and whites at the same income levels. In New York and Columbus, Ohio, the savings of blacks and whites, standardized by their position in the economic distribution for each category, are compared with their average income. At each income level the blacks save more. Keynes's law could not account for the difference in the marginal propensity to save. Duesenberry takes each as a separate community. The black group as a whole is poorer than the white group. Therefore, the percentile position of any black's income in his own group is higher than the percentile position of any white with the same income. Thus, Duesenberry would expect the black, being relatively better off in his own community than his white counterpart, to save more. The reverse is true for professionals versus other social categories in the total population. He quotes a survey in which 11 percent of professional people identify themselves socially with the upper class, and only 5 percent consider themselves economically as upper class. So this would account for their recorded tendency to be dissatisfied with their income at each level, since their percentile position for income would seem relatively low in the population in which they class themselves socially, and

their attempts to meet what they regard as culturally standardized expenditures would always be frustrated by costs.

Beautifully simple as it is, Duesenberry's approach has two
snags. One is that he is led to suppose that savings are always
residual, that the decision to save can only be made after culturally required consumption demands have been met. One
of Charlotte M. Yonge's virtuous heroines, on her marriage to
an unworthy profligate, persuaded him to work out a household budget for her. When he had done so she anxiously re-
marked that he had put nothing aside for charity. For her,
charity was a preempting category, and for him, if it existed,
it was residual. Likewise, Duesenberry ought to recognize that
savings could be a first priority, culturally standardized and imposed. The other snag is his supposition that emulation is the
universal principle dominating consumer behavior. Both shortcomings interlock, since universal competitiveness explains for
Duesenberry why saving is residual. He is content with answering that whereas consumption is visible, savings are hidden.
Consequently, communal pressures to spend now will have
more edge to them than communal pressures to provide for the
future, since the community can see whether the first set of
pressures are being effective and cannot see the savings. But
further reading in ethnography, to say nothing of Max Weber,
shows that many cultures exert a dampening effect on competition. If emulation is not a human universal, his theory rests on
a cultural quirk that happens to be common to Alor and modern
Massachusetts.

Prudence According to Friedman

Economic anthropology could well have provided criticism of
this kind at the time Duesenberry wrote. But anthropologists
were not attending when he fired his salvo. They lost their

turn, and the next big shot fired was by Milton Friedman in 1957.[21] His theory of permanent income is a strictly economic approach, in the sense of assuming that the choice between consumption and saving is made rationally. It needs to assume nothing psychological about emulation and acquisitiveness, nor to make moral judgments between necessary and completely useless categories of consumption. It also does without the concept of culturally distinct populations with culturally derived pressures to consume in standard fashion, which is a pity. Instead it fastens attention on the components of income, transitory or permanent, and the components of capital, human and nonhuman. By analyzing the way income is composed, Friedman is able to explain the same variations in the consumption/savings ratio that Duesenberry explained, and others that Duesenberry could not explain. Friedman assumes that savings are provision for the future, not a residual category. His great contribution, a significant advance over any previous thinker on the subject, is to take the whole life span into his account of the consumer's choices. He assumes that one rational objective for the consumer would be to even out consumption over the life span: if the estimate has worked out well, his reserves will provide him with income from retirement to the grave; if he has underestimated his life expectation and dies too soon, there will be an unplanned legacy for his heirs; if he lives too long, his reserves will run out and he will die in penury. It is an actuary's concept of savings and income. The permanent income hypothesis assumes that the individual has a consumption program for his life, within which he makes his day-to-day budgeting decisions. His life plan shifts all the time as he learns from past experience or as his legitimate expectations change. Thus, there is permanent income and permanent consumption to be understood. Each exists only as a vague guideline in the consumer's mind. The consumer is supposed to be making his decisions with reference to a time horizon, longer for some categories of goods, shorter for others.

Why They Save

It is important to pause here and to consider what a very useful step this approach makes towards an anthropology of consumption. For one thing, the consumer, instead of choosing with no regard to past or future, is credited with an overall objective for his whole life span. The theory is quite flexible enough to allow for communities to impose different patterns of expectation upon their members: one might require each to set aside enough revenue for his own old age and retirement, including a glorious funeral with fireworks and feasting, but nothing for any heirs. Another might expect each to make some hefty bequest or lifetime transfer to children or the Church before retiring to a monastery. The only thing that is necessarily presupposed is that there be a life plan of some kind, and that savings are made out of income from year to year with a view to fulfilling it. Friedman's next important innovation is the idea of permanent consumption. The idea is implicit that consumption involves commitments that cannot be canceled at short notice just because a ship comes in late or the harvest is bad. For this theory, the individual is part of a society, and so borrowing is possible. Permanent income is a term that includes a shorthand reference to wealth, since income is defined as "the amount that a consumer unit believes it could consume while maintaining its wealth intact." [22] Income includes earnings and receipts from holding wealth. For Friedman the most fundamental distinction is between human and nonhuman forms of wealth. Human wealth is the stream of expected future earnings discounted for the present, the capitalized value of these future earnings. The rate of interest at which one can borrow on human capital is likely to be higher than the rate of interest on nonhuman wealth, so the rate of saving will be very different in a community in which the greater proportion of wealth is nonhuman.

Permanent income also depends on the proportion of transitory to permanent items in income and their expected effect on permanent income. An income stream that is made up of a lot of fluctuating and unpredictable transitory items will have to be evened out at a lower level of consumption and with a higher reserve of saving than one in which the permanent elements are in a high proportion. So to estimate permanent consumption, we have to analyze a balance between estimates of human and nonhuman wealth, the proportions of transitory and permanent income, and the ratio of nonhuman wealth to permanent income.

Comparing farm with nonfarm families in the United States between 1935–36 and 1941, Friedman notices that the former fix their normal consumption at a smaller fraction of average income and increase their consumption less rapidly with increases of income. He explains their higher rate of saving from income by their need to even out between good and bad years and by the fact that transitory factors of income loom relatively larger than for nonfarm families. They have more ups and downs due to variations in weather, etc. Income from salaries is more reliable, and so nonfarming families tend to need less smoothing out between one year and another and can pitch higher their normal level of consumption from income. The same applies to the comparison between independent business and fixed salaried classes; Friedman predicts and finds that the independent businesses have a higher savings ratio. These results show that the permanent income theory explains the same data that Duesenberry's theory explains, in addition to other things on which Duesenberry has nothing to say. The figures showing an apparently greater thriftiness of blacks compared with whites (which was important for demonstrating the value of the relative income theory) can be explained now as follows. Black Americans have in general fewer physical assets than whites and are therefore more dependent on human capital than whites. They also have less human capital than whites. The greater difficulty of borrowing on human capital calls for greater prudence and a lower level of consumption. Blacks' life expectations of total wealth or permanent income are much lower. Their spending less than whites at the same level of current measured income would be predicted by the permanent income theory, since it relates current spending and current saving to life expected income and not to current incomes. At any point in the income distribution of whites which matches a point in the income distribution of blacks, the whites can be expected to look forward to a vastly better income in later years and consequently to be currently spending in line with those long-term expectations.

The permanent income theory requires a structural analysis of the whole stream of income: on the two dimensions of transitory versus nontransitory components and human versus nonhuman capital, and within the perspective of the lifetime. The question about whether individuals spend or save windfalls becomes an empty one in much the same way as the old questions of the meaning of a single item of vocabulary or theme in mythology are now shelved in favor of an analysis of the structuring and sequencing of all contrast sets in which they appear. Thus, some famous test cases have not been admitted by Friedman either to test his hypothesis, or to prove or disprove it.[23] If someone gets a large windfall, such as an unexpected bonus or insurance payment, and goes straight out to spend it, his critics have thought that his theory would be disproved, since he predicts that consumption will not be influenced by transitory income. But it all depends on whether they really think it is transitory or a permanent addition to wealth. In his discussion of one such case, Friedman shows the rich demographic and sociological implications of his theory. It cannot be refuted by alleged instances of windfalls which turn out on closer examination to have been anticipated way back or to be regarded as the first of a set of future installments or otherwise incorporated by the recipient into his perception of his permanent income.

A theory that can neither be proved nor refuted by isolated cases, it can only be shown to have strong or weak organizing power. Given the wide range of economies that anthropologists can describe, it is interesting to suggest some of the limits of the theory of consumption. Turning again to the array of social environments encapsulated in our grid-and-group diagram (see figure 2–1), it seems that both Duesenberry and Friedman are working with a concept of human society that fits close to the vertical grid line of the bottom left square. Duesenberry's emulative man, transacting conspicuously with his fellow consumers, is lower down, in a more individualistic, competitive society. Friedman's prudent, farsighted fellow is further up, towards strong grid, harassed by his permanent consumption commitments—mortgage, insurance premiums, perhaps educating his children, perhaps keeping his parents, too—commitments from which he cannot switch funds suddenly from one year to the next. Not surprisingly, both economists place their vision of society within the general assumptions of the market economy. They acknowledge the theory of rationality, which underpins economic theory, the theory of rationality whose emergence to the surface of European moral consciousness Max Weber was engaged in tracing.

But for each of them there is a situation which their theory cannot explain. Duesenberry expects the individuals whose income is well above the average of their society to save most: but when the richest are the most prodigal, he has no explanation to offer. So he can say nothing about the ruinous spending of the great Bordeaux nobility in the Hundred Years' War. Friedman expects the highest rates of savings from the consuming units whose income has the highest proportion of transitory components. His theory cannot explain the thriftlessness, the let-tomorrow-take-care-of-itself, gather-ye-rosebuds attitudes of the laborer, pouring away his transitory income in beer, to the despair of social workers (see chapter 8). The kind of society they each have in mind can be placed on the grid-and-group diagram, rather close together, but the extremes, very strong group, very weak grid, elude their theories.

One reason for stressing the diversity of social environments is to remind the economists that they are seeing human society from a very blinkered viewpoint. The blinkers are their analytic apparatus that places them and the world they see in the left side of the diagram. But the congruence between the analytic principles and their view of the individual is so complete that they cannot see what is missing from the picture. We need a better account of rationality, one that includes the consumer's full range of objectives. We must show how consumption goods enter into the fulfillment of the individual's objectives. Then consumption behavior needs to be anchored to its technological base, so as to establish an objective basis for comparisons of poverty. Finally, we hope to show, too, that questions about poverty and about saving are best answered when the full social dimension is taken into account. If we are indeed committed, by virtue of conditions inherent in the industrial economy, to the individualist environment of weak–grid/weak–group, then the phenomenon of poverty in the midst of plenty will be less paradoxical and mystifying when we understand better what the rich are doing with their goods and their time. We shall see that it is important to know what kind of social environment the rich are generating by their consumption behavior.

Normative Consumption

This presentation of the theory of consumption, highlighting only Duesenberry and Friedman, is the usual way of condensing the history and use of the concept of permanent income in textbooks and review articles.[24] Each contributed a technical improvement to the computations of econometricians. But underlying this methodological advance on a narrow front, there is a history of questioning and research in a much wider context. Since this essay is itself inspired by the idea of a normal or permanent consumption and by the sociological challenge it presents, it is deplorable how many rich ideas in Friedman's *Theory of the Consumption Function* never became algebraized, but instead are bracketed away in the small print and footnotes, ideas which have still not been exploited to the full.

The whole story of the theory of permanent consumption really started in 1934 with Margaret Reid's *Economics of Household Production*.[25] She is a consummate ethnographer and her observations of economic behavior at the level of the household suggested a concept of normal consumption, consisting of commitments which cannot be quickly laid aside once they have been accepted, and consequently which cannot be adjusted to short-term ups and downs of income. She saw each household as an entrepreneurial activity, a firm. Hence her idea—seen in the title of her book—that so-called consumption can be analyzed as a process of production. Then followed the publication of the *Consumers' Purchases Study* (1935–36) and the *Study of Spending and Saving in War-time* (1941–42). It is clear from Dorothy Brady and R. D. Friedman's contribution to the National Bureau of Economic Research volume *Savings and the Income Distribution*[26] that parallel results were being studied and discussed at that time (1947), and that a curiosity had been aroused about the conditions under which household decisions on saving are influenced by the current year or by a longer time span. They show that farm families save more than village families at the same absolute level of income, and conclude that the farmers are behaving more like entrepreneurs. Dr. Klein, commenting in the same volume, concludes that Brady and Friedman have presented "a hypothesis and evidence that the savings ratio is a function of the order position of income in a distribution within a group," a straw in the wind that prepares us for the publication of Duesenberry's *Relative Income Theory* two years later. But already in 1945 the permanent income hypothesis had been stated in Milton Friedman and Simon Kuznet's study of the savings habits of doctors and dentists in the United States, a book rich in sociological insight.[27] In short, there was at that time a great deal of discussion and systematic empirical research into consumption behavior, which presents an impressive contrast with the lightweight airing of worries about the consumer society which is so general now.

Chapter 3

THE USES OF GOODS

Redefining Consumption

To make a fresh start on the subject, an anthropological definition of consumption would help. To speak sensibly of consumption here, in industrial society, in terms that also apply without strain to distant tribal societies that have barely seen commerce, still less capitalism, is indeed a challenge. But unless we make the attempt there can be no anthropology of consumption. We need somehow to extract the essence of the term, while ignoring the potentially misleading local effects. One boundary may be drawn by an idea essential to economic theory: that is, that consumption is not compelled; the consumer's choice is his free choice. He can be irrational, superstitious, traditionalist, or experimental: the essence of the economist's concept of the individual consumer is that he exerts a sovereign choice. Another boundary may be drawn by the idea central to national bookkeeping that consumption starts where market ends. What happens to material objects once they have left the retail outlet and reached the hands of the final purchasers is part of the consumption process. These two boundaries raise various problems and borderline cases for economics and do not make a completely satisfactory definition. Together they assume that consumption is a private matter. Consumption that is provided by government as part of its functioning is not properly part of consumption. Central heating or cups of tea drunk in bureaucratic offices count as part of the cost of administration, in the same way as cups of tea or central heating provided by businesses count as costs of production, not as output, when they make their income tax returns. As to consumption being uncoerced, this is not a straightforward matter either. When a city is proclaimed a smokeless zone by law, householders are not free to burn log fires if they choose; nor are car purchasers free to ignore government regulations as to safety, noise, and so on. But by and large the two boundaries capture the essence of the idea and the detailed tidying-up is a matter of convention. So if we define consumption as a use of material possessions that is beyond commerce and free within the law, we have a concept that travels extremely well, since it fits parallel usages in all those tribes that have no commerce.

Seen under this aspect, consumption decisions become the vital source of the culture of the moment. People who are reared in a particular culture see it change in their lifetime: new words, new ideas, new ways. It evolves and they play a part in the change. Consumption is the very arena in which culture is fought over and licked into shape. The housewife with her shopping basket arrives home: some things in it she reserves for her household, some for the father, some for the children; others are destined for the special delectation of guests. Whom she invites into her house, what parts of the house she makes available to outsiders, how often, what she offers them for music, food, drink, and conversation, these choices express and generate culture in its general sense. Likewise, her husband's judgments as to how much of his wages he allots to her, how much he keeps to spend with his friends, etc., result in the channeling of resources. They vitalize one activity or another. They will be unconstrained if the culture is alive and evolving. Ultimately, they are moral judgments about what a man is, what a woman is, how a man ought to treat his aged parents, how much of a start in life he ought to give his sons and daughters; how he himself should grow old, gracefully or disgracefully, and so on. How many of his aunts and uncles and orphaned nephews is he expected to support? Do family obligations stop him from migrating? Should he contribute to his union? Insure against sickness? Insure for his own funeral? These are consumption choices which may well involve heavy costs, and which, when made, may determine the evolution of culture.

In most cultures reported over the world, there are certain things that cannot be sold or bought. One obvious case with us is political advance (which should not be bought); as to selling, a man who is capable of selling his honor, or even of selling his grandmother, is condemned by cliché. Everywhere there is at least a notion of some area of untrammeled individual choice. If any local tyrant could march into your home, turn out your friends or force you to add unchosen names to your visiting list, tell you whom you can see and speak to and whom to ignore, then personal freedom and dignity would be lost. If he did it by passing laws, by threat of guns, by threat of lost livelihood, he would probably be judged more immoral even than the rich man who might seek to buy your support. We have in fact succeeded in defining consumption as an area of behavior hedged by rules which explicitly demonstrate that neither commerce nor force are being applied to a free relationship.

This is why, no doubt, in our society the line between cash and gift is so carefully drawn. It is all right to send flowers to your aunt in the hospital, but never right to send the cash they are worth with a message to "get yourself some flowers"; all right to offer lunch or drinks, but not to offer the price of a lunch or a drink. Hosts may go to extravagant lengths to attract and please guests—short of offering them money to come to the party. Social sanctions protect the boundary. Apparently, some fabled New York hostess in the 1890s, worrying how to surpass her rival who habitually gave each guest a rich jewel, was worried even more by their derision when, her turn having come, she folded a crisp $100 bill in each napkin. The right to give cash is reserved for family intimacy. Here again there are details that could be tidied up. But in general it is true to say that around the field of consumption we have a spontaneous, operative boundary between two kinds of services: professional, paid with money and to be classed with commerce, and personal, recompensed in kind and in no other way. Within the field of personal services, freely given and returned, moral judgment of the worth of people and things is exercised. This establishes the first step in a cultural theory of consumption.

A Universe Constructed from Commodities

Instead of supposing that goods are primarily needed for subsistence plus competitive display, let us assume that they are needed for making visible and stable the categories of culture. It is standard ethnographic practice to assume that all material possessions carry social meanings and to concentrate a main part of cultural analysis upon their use as communicators.

In every tribal study an account is given of the material parts of the culture. Like us, the members of a tribe have fixed equipment, houses, gardens, barns, and like us, they have durable and nondurable things. The anthropologist usually devotes some space to marshaling the evidence for deciding, from the vantage point of our technology, whether, for example, the cattle husbandry is efficient, the farmer's knowledge of his soils and seasons accurate, the hygienic precautions and the amount of food taken adequate, etc. The material possessions provide food and covering, and this has to be understood. But at the same time it is apparent that the goods have another important use: they also make and maintain social relationships. This is a long-tried and fruitful approach to the material side of existence which yields a much richer idea of social meanings than mere individual competitiveness.

A well-known case is Evans-Pritchard's account of the place of cattle in Nuer lives:

The network of kinship ties which links members of local communities is brought about by the operation of exogamous rules, often stated in terms of cattle. The union of marriage is brought about by the payment of cattle and every phase of the ritual is marked by their transference or slaughter. The legal status of the partners is defined by cattle rights and obligations.

Cattle are owned by families. When the head of the household is alive he has full rights of disposal over the herd, though his wives have rights of use in the cows and his sons own some of the oxen. As each son, in order of seniority, reaches the age of marriage he marries with cows from the herd. The next son will have to wait till the herd has reached its earlier strength before he can marry in his turn. . . . The bond of cattle between brothers is continued long after each has a home and children of his own, for when a daughter of any one of them is married the others receive a large portion of her bride-wealth. Her grandparents, maternal uncles, paternal and maternal aunts, and even more distant relatives also receive a portion. Kinship is customarily defined by reference to these payments, being most clearly pointed at marriage, when movements of cattle from kraal to kraal are equivalent to lines in a genealogical chart. It is also emphasized by division of sacrificial meat among agnatic and cognatic relatives. . . . Nuer tend to define all social processes and relationships in terms of cattle. Their social idiom is a bovine idiom.[1]

This approach to goods, emphasizing their double role in providing subsistence and in drawing the lines of social relationships, is agreed upon, practically axiomatic among anthropologists, as the way to a proper understanding of why people need goods. But there are some problems about transferring the insight to our own ethnography of ourselves.

Each branch of the social sciences has been bogged down

until it has drawn a distinctive line between the level of human behavior that its techniques are adapted to analyze and all other levels. Durkheim, for example, required the identification of "social facts" by his rules of method.[2] Each such isolation of a part or layer of the social process is a self-denying ordinance, an austerity, practiced for the sake of learning not to pose unanswerable questions. Of course there is always a loss of richness, which the gains in clarity have to justify. Long before Durkheim, economists had carved out a sphere of "economic facts" by disregarding the ends of human activity and concentrating on problems of choice. The history of anthropology has been one of continual disengagement of theoretical fields from the intrusive assumptions from common sense. In each case enlightenment has followed a decision to ignore the physiological levels of existence which sustain the behavior in question. For interpreting bizarre kinship terminologies it was at first assumed that the clue to the uses of the terms "Father" and "Mother" would lie in some long-abandoned arrangements for marriage and procreation. No advance was made until kinship terms were cut free from their obvious biological meanings and seen as constituting a system for organizing social relations —a system based on the metaphors of engendering and rearing. In turn, Lévi-Strauss made a similar stand when he ridiculed the idea that the origin of totemism was some gastronomic criterion that reserved the most delicious foods to privileged persons. Animals which are tabooed are chosen, he said, because they are good to think, not because they are good to eat. So he was able to reveal a systematic relation between natural and human species as the typical basis of primitive thought.[3] Again, as another example, in nineteenth-century comparative religion, medical materialism blocked the interpretation of ideas about the contagiousness of magic. Scholars were sidetracked by occasional signs of medical benefit following rites of purification. But it can be argued that these rites are better understood as being concerned with making visible the boundaries between cognitive categories than with pathogenicity in the strict medical sense.[4] Now we are trying the same exercise with consumption goods, bracketing away for the moment their practical uses. If it is said that the essential function of language is its capacity for poetry, we shall assume that the essential function of consumption is its capacity to make sense. Forget the idea of consumer irrationality. Forget that commodities are good for eating, clothing, and shelter; forget their usefulness and try instead the idea that commodities are good for thinking; treat them as a nonverbal medium for the human creative faculty.

Theoretical Individualism

The time is ripe for this new approach. Individualist theories of knowledge and behavior have had their day and run their course. Here and there the outposts are still manned. Perhaps Peter Blau is one of the most forceful exponents of the eighteenth-century tradition (to which economics as a whole is heir). The Benthamite view of human psychology starts and ends with the individual agent. Other people appear only insofar as they may help or hinder his life project. He can use or be used by them, but they lurk always in a shadow cast by his egocentric awareness. Blau's theory of social structure tried to build up society from the simplest relations between individuals. He concedes that most pleasures have their roots in social life: "There is something pathetic about the person who derives his major gratifications from food and drink as such, since it reveals either excessive need or excessive greed, the pauper, . . . the glutton." [5] Anyway, there are no simple processes in the relations between individuals. They can only be postulated arbitrarily, and so Blau's focus upon power is itself an arbitrary and biased restriction: "The satisfaction a man derives from exercising power over others requires that they endure the deprivation of being subject to his power; . . . individuals associate with one another because they all profit from the association. But they do not necessarily all profit equally, nor do they share the cost of providing the benefits equally. . . ." And so onward to a theory of individualistic social exchange. Blau stands in a low grid/low group position, where the view of a world organized as a competitive, power-seeking game between individuals has *a priori* rightness. His work is a rescue job, salvaging an approach whose reverberations will appeal automatically to other thinkers who also share the same standpoint. But the anthropologist can recognize this approach itself as an example of a cultural bias rooted in a certain kind of social experience. Other cultural biases derive from other social forms. Our ultimate task is to find interpretative procedures that will uncover each bias and discredit its claims to universality. When this is done the eighteenth century can be formally closed, and a new era that has been here a long time can be officially recognized.

The individual human being, stripped of his humanity, is of no use as a conceptual base from which to make a picture of human society. No human exists except steeped in the culture of his time and place. The falsely abstracted individual has been sadly misleading to Western political thought.[6] But now we can start again at a point where major streams of thought converge, at the other end, at the making of culture. Cultural analysis sees the whole tapestry as a whole, the picture and the weaving process, before attending to the individual threads.

At least three intellectual positions being developed today encourage such an approach. One, the philosophical movement styled Phenomenology started by taking seriously the question of our knowledge of other persons. It sets the individual squarely in a social context, treating knowledge as a joint constructive enterprise. Knowledge is never a matter of the lone individual learning about an external reality. Individuals interacting together impose their constructions upon reality: the world is socially constructed.[7]

Structuralism is a convergent movement whose implicit theory of knowledge transcends the efforts of the individual thinker, and focuses upon social processes in knowledge. In its many forms, modern structural analysis, the offspring of the electronic computer, affords possibilities of interpreting culture and of relating cultural to social forms, possibilities that outpace any approaches that doggedly start with the individual.[8]

And finally, closest to the present task, is the Californian movement in sociology called "social accounting" or ethnomethodology. This takes it for granted that reality is socially constructed and also takes it for granted that reality can be analyzed as logical structures in use. It focuses on interpretative procedures—on the methods of verification used by listeners, methods of proving credibility used by speakers, on the whole system of accountability which operates in everyday life.[9] Their approach to the testing and confirming of information starts from the idea that meaning is embedded, that it is never easily picked from the surface of a communication. Speech is only one channel, and speech itself does not make sense unless it matches the information that is scanned by the hearer from the physical demeanor and surroundings of the speaker—spacing, timing, orientation, clothing, food, and so on. And, of course, this has to include goods. Though for the present it focuses on procedures of interpretation, for its further development this approach will certainly need to turn to cultural analysis. For culture is a possible pattern of meanings inherited from the immediate past, a canopy for the interpretative needs of the present.

Fixing Public Meanings

But what is meaning? It flows and drifts; it is hard to grasp. Meaning tacked to one set of clues transforms itself. One person gets one pattern and another a quite different one from the same events; seen a year later they take a different aspect again. The main problem of social life is to pin down meanings so that they stay still for a little time. Without some conventional ways of selecting and fixing agreed meanings, the minimum consensual basis of society is missing. As for tribal society, so too for us: rituals serve to contain the drift of meanings. Rituals are conventions that set up visible public definitions. Before the initiation there was a boy, after it a man; before the marriage rite there were two free persons, after it two joined as one. Before admission to a hospital, the doctor's certificate of ill health; before the formal declaration of death, the dead is accounted alive; before the body is found, no murder charge sticks; without formal testimony, slander is not slander; without a witnessed signature, the deceased's last will is not valid. To manage without rituals is to manage without clear meanings and possibly without memories. Some are purely verbal rituals, vocalized, unrecorded, but they fade on the air and hardly help to limit the interpretative scope. More effective rituals use material things, and the more costly the ritual trappings, the stronger we can assume the intention to fix the meanings to be. Goods, in this perspective, are ritual adjuncts; consumption is a ritual process whose primary function is to make sense of the inchoate flux of events.

From here it is a short step to the identification of the overall objective that rational beings, by definition, can be supposed to set themselves. Their own rationality must press them to make sense of their environment. The most general objective of the consumer can only be to construct an intelligible universe with the goods he chooses. How does this cognitive construction proceed? To start with, a social universe needs a demarcated temporal dimension. The calendar has to be notched for annual, quarterly, monthly, weekly, daily and shorter periodicities. The passage of time can then be laden with meaning. The calendar gives a principle for rotation of duties, for establishing precedence, for review and renewal. Another year passed, a new beginning; 25 years, a silver jubilee; 100, 200 years, a centennial or bicentennial celebration; there is a time for living and a time for dying, a time for loving. Consumption goods are used for notching off these intervals: their range in quality arises from the need to differentiate through the calendar year and the life cycle.

This argument does not deny that there is such a thing as private enjoyment. It is developed to assert a straight analytic need to recognize how enjoyment is structured and how much it owes to social standardization. Those who fancy a simple life, with only enough goods for a modest subsistence, should try to imagine a standardized meal, say breakfast, served at all mealtime slots in the weekday, at all meals in the week, at all meals in the year including Christmas Day and Thanksgiving. Food is a medium for discriminating values, and the more numerous the discriminated ranks, the more varieties of food will be needed. The same for space. Harnessed to the cultural process, its divisions are heavy with meaning: housing, size, the side of the street, distance from other centers, special limits, all shore up conceptual categories. The same for clothing, transport, and sanitation; they afford sets of markers within the spatial and temporal frame. The choice of goods continuously creates certain patterns of discrimination, overlaying or reinforcing others. Goods, then, are the visible part of culture. They are arranged in vistas and hierarchies that can give play to the full range of discrimination of which the human mind is capable. The vistas are not fixed: nor are they randomly arranged in a kaleidoscope. Ultimately, their structures are anchored to human social purposes.

Hearing this, the economist usually asks: what about the solitary consumer? The man who feeds alone can hardly be said to be sustaining a universe of meanings; the man who reads or listens to music alone, goes for walks alone, what of his consumption of books and shoeleather? The answer comes in three parts. Admittedly, there is a class of solitary feeding, where the person wolfs or bolts his food, probably standing by his refrigerator in his overcoat; this should count as part of a private hygiene, in the same way as his use of soap and toothbrushes. Private hygiene is probably a small item in the sum of consumption goods. But even so, if a person normally chooses his soap and pares his nails for entirely nonsocial reasons the advertising industry is wildly wrong. The lonely walks may count as private hygiene, too, as long as the walker never shares his experience by speaking or writing about it. But the music is another matter. The music lover presumably knows a lot about music and is observing the fine discrimination and shifts of practice that are the history of music; he may even be passing judgment (albeit privately) on whether one performance is better than another. He is sharing in an intensely social, cultural process. So, too, is the solitary eater who unthinkingly adopts the sequential rules and categories of the wider society; the man who uses a butter knife when he is alone, even if he doesn't dress for dinner. He would never reverse the conventional sequence, beginning with pudding and ending with soup, or eat mustard with lamb or mint with beef. We may reckon his observance of the rules followed by other consumers as a way of keeping him in practice, or perhaps as a memorial rite. If the gastric juices flow best when the meal is well constructed, well served, and enjoyed in good company, the solitary consumer may be helping his own digestion by adopting the social criteria. But he is certainly helping to uphold the latter. In general, the case of the solitary consumer is a weak counter to the argument that consumption activity is the joint production, with fellow consumers, of a universe of values. Consumption uses goods to make firm and visible a particular set of judgments in the fluid processes of classifying persons and events. We have now defined it as a ritual activity.

But the individual needs compliant fellows if he is to succeed in changing the public categories, reducing their disorder and making the universe more intelligible. His project of creating intelligibility depends heavily on them. He must ensure their attending his rituals and inviting him to theirs. By their freely given presence he obtains a judgment from them of the fitness of the choice he makes of consumer goods for celebrating particular occasions and a judgment on his own relative standing as a judge, as well as a judgment on the fitness of the occasion to be celebrated. Within the available time and space the individual uses consumption to say something about himself, his family, his locality, whether in town or country, on vacation or at home. The kind of statements he makes are about the kind of universe he is in, affirmatory or defiant, perhaps competitive, but not necessarily so. He can proceed, through consumption activities, to get agreement from fellow consumers to redefine some traditional events as major that used to be minor, and to allow others to lapse completely. In England, Guy Fawkes Day comes forward where Halloween used to be. Christmas overshadows New Year in England but not in Scotland, and Mother's Day still hovers on the brink of recognition. The same for the decoration of the home and even the constitution of a meal. Consumption is an active process in which all the social categories are being continually redefined.

For anthropologists the word potlatch sums up this characteristic of feasting, inviting guests, and competing in hospitable honors. There are many variants of the potlatch described in American Northwest Coast ethnography. A Skagit Indian described the potlatch as "shaking hands in a material way." For these Indians of Puget Sound,

the activities of the food cycle and the social season of a single year are posited in socio-religious theory. The cumulative successes and failures of many years were expressed in winter ceremonials. Although a usually prosperous village might have had such a poor summer that its headman could afford few extravagances in the next winter, his success in past winters would nevertheless be commemorated in potlatches, with the attitude that his bad luck was only temporary and that he would recover from his debts in another season. Only repeated misfortune, of several consecutive years, would reduce his standing enough to alter potlatch behavior toward him. He would postpone potlatching, and hopefully he would avoid loss of status by announcing his obligations on public occasions. Although his demeanor did not convey embarrassment or humility, his words did, expressing an apologetic, almost cringingly guilty attitude about his bad luck. In grandiose language he, or more usually a hired spokesman, extolled the generosity of the guests and compared it with his own feeble though well-meant efforts to be the same. Because the source of bad luck was invariably bad behavior, and because good men were honest men, it was necessary that he publicly confess and then promise to reform. But a potlatch leader's confessions and resolutions usually were masked in generalities. He merely alluded to a misdeed that he thought might have become known to his audience. He did not specify who did what or exactly what he as a chief was going to do about it. And his humble words were punctuated by even more elaborate oratory reminding the assemblage of the brilliance of his own past and that of his ancestors. Such a performance was the ultimate expression of upper-class dignity in the face of adversity. A good reputation, mere words of condescension, and a defensive attitude could sustain even a faltering career among the Skagit for quite some years.

While upper-class men lost status gradually as a result of a series of economic set-backs, chiefs in newly formed villages, descendants of commoners, were but grudgingly admitted to one or another potlatch circle as important invited guests. Especially if they had suddenly become rich, they were looked upon as conniving vulgarians without right to such good fortune. Their wealth would be overlooked at give-aways sponsored by hosts of the old guard, who contemptuously identified them, instead, with their former anonymity. And when the *arrivistes* pretentiously potlatched, their betters, the elite who mattered, would not acknowledge invitations. A potlach of this kind was a fiasco. The etiquette of potlatching made it almost impossible for untested claimants to high station to crash the society of Skagit bluebloods. Unless a new village had steadily grown in numbers and prosperity over a generation or two, during which time its leaders had maintained a mock servility on public occasions, it would never come to be accepted by old, influential villages as a worthy rival. One way by which the Skagit publicly expressed respect for other families and communities was to allow them to compete on the same footing. Trust in people of proven, established lineage, and scorn and fear of Johnnies-come-lately had a sound practical basis, according to Skagit rationalizations about social class behavior. *Nouveaux riches* potlatchers lacked training for the manipulation of wealth and were liable to provoke, intentionally or unintentionally, embarrassing situations. That is, they might insult the pride of their august guests, which would only have to be avenged to no one's particular social or economic advantage. They were not to be trusted on general principles. Most had reputations for filial impiety, because their leadership was of recent origin and was due to the disloyalty of an ancestor (of several generations ago) and his break with his parental village to found a new one.[10]

Surely we can see here a parallel to the way in which we ourselves proceed to fix or to challenge public meanings.

Chapter 4

EXCLUSION, INTRUSION

Goods as Material Culture

To keep sane, there is a minimal objective which, by definition, the rational individual must seek for his lifetime. The concept of economic rationality says nothing anywhere about any general objective of the individual. Hicks, who did so much to purge demand theory of unwarranted psychology, drew attention to this gap:

we ought to think of the consumer as choosing according to his prefrences, between certain objectives; in deciding, more or less as the entrepreneur decides, between alternative means of reaching these objectives. The commodities which he purchases are for the most part means to the attainment of objectives, not objectives themselves.[1]

The need to be able to choose rationally in an intelligible world is simply an extension of the concept of economic rationality. Without it, all the other assumptions of the concept amount to very little. All other living beings submit their experience to a species-specific organizing framework that limits the scope of possible messages and responses. But human rationality does not submit. It negotiates the organizing structures. Human experience can flow into a vast variety of possible frameworks, for the rational human is responsible for continually recreating a universe in which choice can take place. Making sense of the world involves interpreting the world as sensible. Once this has been conceded, the question of why people want goods can shift into something like an information approach. But it is a rather different exercise from the economic analysis that counts the cost of information as part of the cost of production. In that case the messages about prices and wages are seen as moving through a fixed information system. But consumption goods are most definitely not mere messages; they constitute the very system itself. Take them out of human intercourse and you have dismantled the whole thing. In being offered, accepted, or refused, they either reinforce or undermine existing boundaries. The goods are both the hardware and the software, so to speak, of an information system whose principal concern is to monitor its own performance.

This stroke dissolves the Cartesian dichotomy between physical and psychic experience. Goods that minister to physical needs—food or drink—are no less carriers of meaning than ballet or poetry. Let us put an end to the widespread and misleading distinction between goods that sustain life and health and others that service the mind and heart—spiritual goods. That false distinction leaves a mass of unnecessary luxuries to be accounted for by a mixture of consumer gullibility and sinister advertising.[2] The counterargument proposed here is that all goods carry meaning, but none by itself. Just as one gesture of saving cannot be interpreted by itself, but only as part of the whole perceived flow of income throughout the lifetime, and just as one word from a poem used in another context has no poetry, so one physical object has no meaning by itself, and the question of why it is valued has no meaning either. The meaning is in the relations between all the goods, just as music is in the relations marked out by the sounds and not in any one note.

Brillat-Savarin considered champagne to be a stimulant in its first effects, but stupefying at the later stages. Roland Barthes feels that this would apply better to whisky than to champagne.[3] As champagne or whisky have their first and second effects, some speech develops meanings after the sound of the words has died away. According to Brillat-Savarin the principles that govern gastronomic taste recognize multiple and successive experiences. Gustation makes a pattern from the palate's experience of entries, returns, detours; it has a whole counterpoint of sensation, ending only with the final judgment. So where is the physical and where the intellectual aspect of eating food? And, one might well ask, where is its metaphysical aspect? Apparently Baudelaire reproached Brillat-Savarin for not having said the right things about wine. To Baudelaire, wine was memory and oblivion, happiness and melancholy; it was a drug that could transport one out of oneself into strange and deviant states. But Brillat-Savarin never considered wine as a means to ecstasy. Wine was part of nourishment, and nourishment was for him essentially convivial. It was impossible, then, to think of wine as inducing a private experience. Drinking is part of eating and eating is always social; even during eating, the meal is subject to community rule, to conversation. Conversation regulates culinary joys within a healthy rationality. So, far from according any special privilege to wine, as a drug serving ends other than nourishment, Brillat-Savarin prescribed wine as an antidrug.[4] Scratch underneath any disagreement on tastes and far-reaching metaphysical differences may be revealed, such as those between the poet and the physician on the uses of wine. Even the choice of kitchen utensils is anchored to deep preconceptions about man and nature. To borrow more from Roland Barthes's discussion, take the process of making coffee: you can use a pestle and mortar or a mechanical grinder. Brillat-Savarin preferred coffee beans pounded by hand in Turkish fashion, and gave several practical and theoretical reasons. But beyond these, Barthes discerns a poetic bias; the grinder works mechanically, the human hand only supplies force, and electric power can easily be substituted for it; its produce is a kind of dust—fine, dry, and impersonal. By contrast, there is an art in wielding the pestle. Bodily skills are involved, and the stuff on which they are bestowed is not hard metal, but instead the noblest of materials, wood. And out of the mortar comes not a mere dust, but a gritty powder, pointing straight to the ancient lore of alchemy and its potent brews. The choice between pounding and grinding is thus a choice between two different views of the human condition and between metaphysical judgments lying just beneath the surface of the question.[5] Market researchers know this hidden area well enough, and exploit it for their limited purposes. But to incorporate it in economic theory is a more difficult exploitation of implicit knowledge.

Marking Services

The procedure that could map something of this subterranean field of choice would deliberately rule out, as an unnecessary distraction, the physical uses of goods. Scientists suspend everyday knowledge and create pockets of disbelief.[6] We can suspend our knowledge that goods serve bodily needs and focus instead on the classifying project to which they are recruited. Treat the goods then as markers, the visible bit of the iceberg which is the whole social process. Goods are used for marking in the sense of classifying categories. Marking is the right word here. It draws on the meanings of the hallmarking of gold and silver and pewter; the signing by unlettered persons of their intentions; the authenticating of work; marking in the schoolroom, where performances are judged alpha, beta, gamma;

marking by setting up milestones, parish boundaries; anointing with oil; and marking with ashes, brands, and benchmarks of all kinds. There may be private marking, but here we refer to a public use. Goods are endowed with value by the agreement of fellow consumers. They come together to grade events, upholding old judgments or reversing them. Each person is a source of judgments and a subject of judgments; each individual is in the classification scheme whose discriminations he is helping to establish. By the presence of his fellows at his family funerals and weddings, by their regard for his birthdays, in their visits to his sickbed, they render marking services to him. The kind of world they create together is constructed from commodities that are chosen for their fitness to mark the events in an appropriately graded scale. Goods perish or are consumed, but this is a small part of the total consumption process. In the light of an information approach, it will seem arbitrary to define goods by the itemized market transactions that deliver them into the home. Each item can equally be perceived as a mere installment, just part of a flow of marking tape or paint that goes into the construction of a classification system. The stream of consumable goods leaves a sediment that builds up the structure of culture like coral islands. The sediment is the learned set of names and names of sets, operations to be performed upon names, a means of thinking.

Enjoyment of physical consumption is only a part of the service yielded by goods; the other part is the enjoyment of sharing names. Take any sport, tennis for instance: some people actually play it, some go to Wimbledon, others watch on television. Take football, or cricket: the fan internalizes a reel of his names inside his head. He knows the famous victories, infamous losses, and draws; he loves to talk about historic games, good referees, vast crowds, inspiring captains, good years and bad, the present and the old days. Inside him are grades of passionate judgment. Another enthusiast need only utter two words to betray the vast amount of sharing that is possible for them both. These joys of sharing names are the rewards of a long investment of time and attention and also of cash. The actual physical outlay that makes new names flow into the collection can be called "proving." The proof of a pudding is in the eating. If no one ever ate the food or saw the football match, there would be no way of judging one opinion truer than another. Physical consumption allows proving, testing, or demonstrating that the experience in question is feasible. But the anthropological argument insists that by far the greater part of utility is yielded not at proving but in sharing names that have been learned and graded. This is culture.

We have used naming as a useful ploy for shifting the view of consumption from goods to culture and for insisting that any choice between goods is the result of, and contributes to, culture. In the end we shall be obliged to return to studying prices and incomes almost as if names had never been introduced. Names are an aspect of consumption too intellectual and too abstract to yield to the crude tools of sociological investigation. But the questions we shall examine as responses to changes in incomes and prices of goods will be new ones. For by a proper dealing with rational activity, the theory of demand will have been clarified by the idea of the individual's commitment to an intelligible universe.

Problems of Synthesis

In the last resort the judgment upon culture rests on two criteria. One depends upon scale, whether the knowledge being judged is extensive or small; the other depends on integration of the knowledge. Both are important, but somehow extent of information is not impressive unless the pieces of information assembled are integrated into a general viewpoint. This bias reflects the marketability of the knowledge. Mr. Memory, however incredible the range of facts at his fingertips, cannot deliver a wise opinion. In our language the cultured person has made of what he knows a synthesis so complete that his behavior implies a natural mastery. Anthony Trollope, who reflected much on these things, is a splendid source of illustration for this theme. He discusses at length whether being a gentleman means being a "man of ancestry," a man of professional standing, or a man of good taste in matters of consumption: someone was judged well-dressed

who looks always as if he had been sent home in a bandbox . . . never, at any moment,—going into the city or coming out of it, on horseback or on foot, at home over his book or after the mazes of the dance—was he dressed otherwise than with perfect care. Money and time did it, but folk thought it grew with him, as did his hair and nails. . . ." [7]

This for Trollope would be the final test: culture should fit, not like a glove, but like a skin. The fake could be bought, but true culture he saw as a synthesis that had to grow naturally.

This impression of natural culture would be the result of continuous synthesis over a broad front. Using consumption to mark an internal process of classification, in our theory the individual must seek both scope and synthesis. The wider the net his classifications fling over the manifold of experience, the greater the initial difficulties of relating different fields meaningfully—the more like a glove, the less like a skin. But if classification proceeds within a finite universe, eventually benefits of scale will accrue. Meanings acquired here can be extended there, and the same classes of people can be seen performing similar functions in different contexts. It would be like reaching the top peaks of a mountain range after seeing the lower levels gradually brought within the field of vision. The meanings from one realm of discourse play back upon the others. In the finite social world, securely bounded, the meanings fold back, echo, and reinforce one another: each additional field is brought under rational control more easily by virtue of something like economies of scale. Really worthwhile economies of scale become apparent when consumption is seen as part of an information system operating between rather than within households, and when the consumer's main objective is to gain or keep control of the sources of information so that his own rational interpretations are secure.

Now we can begin to understand the driving force behind demand. The rational individual must seek as large a scale of operation as needful for the synthesis of what he knows. He continually needs to maintain his synthesis or adapt it in the light of rival views. The risk for him comes from an alien view that is more comprehensive in scope than his own. Thus seen, his concerns are a direct reflection of the division of labor in the productive side of the economy. As producers seek benefits of scale to lower costs of production, they expand the horizons of knowledge and force consumers to do likewise. On this view, the rational individual seeking information is not necessarily seeking to control other people, nor are his proclivities necessarily gregarious. Rather, the other way, it could be one of the advantages of a large income to be able to get the classifications confirmed and learn new names with the minimum of inconvenient social intercourse. An example is Lord Egremont, a very rich man, to whom we owe Turner's great pictures of Petworth:

Lord Egremont liked to have people there who he was certain would not put him out of his way, especially those who, entering into his eccentric habits, were ready for the snatches of talk which his perpetual locomotion alone admitted of, and from whom he could gather information about passing events; but it was necessary to conform to his peculiarities and these were utterly incompatible with conversation, or any prolonged discussion. He never remained for 5 minutes in the same place, and was continually oscillating between the library and his bedroom, or wandering about the enormous house in all directions: sometimes he broke off in the middle of a conversation on some subject which appeared to interest him, and disappeared, and an hour after, on a casual meeting, would resume just where he had left off.[8]

This is an example of someone using his great wealth to get "information about passing events" without involving himself in even the inconvenience of staying in the same room till the end of the conversation.

An information approach to demand would imply that the individual is behaving rationally to get the best information that is available, and to get near its sources so as to have it reliably and quickly. A surer way to prevent his own sanity being overwhelmed by other people's contrary interpretations is to take charge of the information himself, for information is continuously developed and transformed by fellow humans. To interpret it he should be where it is being processed and contribute to the processing. Otherwise, his project to make sense of the universe is jeopardized when rival interpretations gain more currency than his own, and the cues that he uses become useless because others have elaborated a different set and put it into circulation.

This is precisely how David Knowles draws the contrast between the fate of the Black Monks as they declined in thirteenth-century England and that of the Friars as they rose to eminence at the same time.[9] After the first great Plague, depopulation led to a rise in labor costs, but no compensating rise in the prices of corn and wool. The Augustinians, the Black Monks, long and successfully established in farming and commerce, managed to adjust to the new conditions, withdrawing from direct control of the land and drawing their income from rents. One way and another they conserved or even increased their immense wealth, but they cut the links with the life of the nation which held them in the forefront of its culture. Earlier they had written the literature and history and were leaders in thought, but in the thirteenth century they gradually dropped out and were replaced by the Friars and secular scholars trained in the schools. In David Knowles's analysis, their loss of control of the information system underlies the other symptoms that pointed to a not very distant disaster.

By contrast, as the Black Monks were consolidating their riches and retreating from the mainstream of English intellectual life, the Friars Minor moved in and took over, with an utterly different outlook. They eschewed possessions, denying themselves even corporate property, but they very deliberately and systematically took over the channels of information.

Nine ragged beggars arrived at Dover in 1224. In six months they had made permanent settlements in Canterbury, London, and Oxford, choosing the ecclesiastical, civil, and intellectual centers of English life. In the course of the next twelve years they made settlements in all the principal towns of the central parallelogram of England. Twenty years after their arrival there were Friars settled at both university towns, fifteen of the nineteen cathedral cities, and in twenty-five of the towns which eventually became cathedral towns. From there they dominated the intellectual and spiritual life of their day.

How to transfer these institutional experiences to those of individual consumers needs some thought. The decisions referred to in the case of the Black Monks, decisions to become rent-collecting landlords, are decisions about the income-earning part of their life. Decisions to settle in the main centers, in the case of the Friars, may be counted equally as decisions about work and about consumption. Some individual choices, whether about choice of work or choice of residence, lead the chooser to be better hooked up or more cut off from the ever-changing mainstream of society. Gabriel Tarde was a sociologist sympathetic to this approach, since he argued that political power depends on inventiveness and the ability to launch inventions and get them widely accepted. "We have seen that the true, basic sources of power are propagated by discoveries or inventions." [10] Here we come very close to the new approaches to international trade, emphasizing innovation and new technology, which turn out to be very helpful in later chapters. Tarde made no difference between control of information as a source of power and as a means of avoiding decline. If we follow him, we have come several steps beyond defining the individual rational consumer. First we supposed the rational individual must interpret his universe as intelligible; then we argued that he needed the services of other people to affirm and stabilize its intelligibility and that goods are a medium for eliciting that consensus. Now we have to raise the question of his power to attract and hold their collaboration, the question of control.

Strategies of Intrusion

If we use "names" as handles for grasping the more hidden cognitive processes synthesizing consumption, and if we view goods and their names as the accessible parts of an information system, the consumer's problem in achieving his life-project becomes clearer. He needs goods to give marking services and to get marking services; that is, he has to be present at other people's rituals of consumption to be able to circulate his own judgments of the fitness of the things used to celebrate the diverse occasions. But economic and political forces may restrict the circle of guests. Trollope gives the lie to those economists who believe that human nature is entirely governed by competitive display. In certain conditions, true emulation is a dominant motive, but in others he describes, it is completely absent: for example, the secure society of the landed gentry, the great professions, and the aristocracy. For the people at the fringes of these islands of stable wealth, there are no prospects of money, income, or standing except by making a rich marriage; these are people very short of names.

It is certainly a service to a man to know who were his grandfathers and who were his grandmothers if he entertain an ambition to move in the upper circles of society, and also of service to be able to speak of them as of persons who had been themselves somebodies in their time. . . .

No publicity agent could be more aware of the advantage of being seen in the right places than were the Hittaways:

Mr. Hittaway could name to you three or four men holding responsible permanent official posts quite as good as his own . . . but they were simply head clerks and nothing more. Nobody knew anything of them. They had no names. You did not meet them anywhere. Cabinet Ministers had never heard of them. . . . The names of Mr. and Mrs. Hittaway were constantly in the papers. They were invited to evening gatherings "up the river," etc., and so they also went to Scotland. "A great many people go to Scotland in the autumn. When you have your autumn holiday in hand to dispose of it, there is nothing more aristocratic you can do than go to Scotland. Dukes are more plentiful there than in Pall Mall, and you will meet an earl or at least a lord on every mountain. Of course if you merely travel about from inn to inn, and neither have a moor of your own or stay with any great friend, you don't quite enjoy the cream of it." [11]

Running like a refrain through the lives of these shadowy figures with no lands and no relatives is the question of their guest lists. Lizzie Eustace, the ambitious widow, decided to exercise hospitality in her Scottish castle. But there were problems in getting the best assortment of guests.

She wrote even to her husband's uncle, the bishop, asking him down to Portray. He could not come, but sent an affectionate answer, and thanked her for thinking of him. Many people she asked who, she felt sure, would not come,—and one or two of them accepted her invitation. John Eustace promised to be with her for two days.

To her cousin she made a special plea: "Come to me just for a week, when my people are here, so that I may not seem to be deserted. Sit at the bottom of my table, and be to me as a brother might. I shall expect you to do so much for me." [12] Apart from her cousin and brother-in-law, she managed to assemble only very dubious guests, each hoping for some profitable adventure.

An impressive guest list was by no means easy to secure. The rich old lawyer, Mr. Wharton, no sooner entered a room than the first scanning of it would tell him whether the company was good or not: "What a very vulgar set of people!" he would be apt to comment.[13] This, after Mrs. Roby had assembled Sir Damask and Lady Monogram, people moving in the highest circles, and Lord Mongrober, "a lord—an absolute peer of Parliament!" She had brought it off mainly by her knowledge of food and wine:

The Mongrober estates were not supposed to be large, nor was the Mongrober influence at this time extensive. But this nobleman was seen about a good deal in society when the dinners were supposed to be worth eating. . . . [He was] a gentleman who said very little, and who when he did speak seemed always to be in an ill-humour. He would now and then make ill-natured remarks about his friends' wines, as suggesting '68 when a man would boast of his '48 claret,— and when costly dainties were set before him would remark that such and such a dish was very well at some other time of the year. So that ladies attentive to their tables and hosts proud of their wines would almost shake in their shoes before Lord Mongrober. And it may be said that Lord Mongrober never gave any chance of retaliation by return dinners. There lived not the man or woman who had dined with Lord Mongrober.[14]

Lord Mongrober is a very interesting case for the anthropology of consumption. Apparently the marking services that his hosts rendered to him by inviting him to share their celebrations needed no repayment beyond his mere presence. The incivilities they endured at his hands were well balanced by the benefit he bestowed by tasting their food and not throwing it back in their faces. His mere presence was a signal to everyone that the feast was superb; his expertise made him into a kind of superconsumer whose good marks were more valued than those of the ordinary run of guests. In a recent interview in a Sunday paper, a London museum director averred that though he was out every evening and booked up three weeks ahead, he never entertained. He too must be offering some kind of reciprocal marking services. Let us hope that the comments he makes on the authenticity of his hosts' antiques are more generous than Mongrober's on the gastronomic arts.

It is not very likely that the Mongrobers of this world flourish in every kind of society. A problematic guest list is not necessarily the normal social predicament. However, it is notable that in a parable in St. Matthew's Gospel, God himself is drawn as a host who has trouble in assembling his chosen guests. Some make excuses and fail to turn up, others insult his messengers, so he forces into service a very mixed assembly, and then, rather unfairly, is harsh to one who is incorrectly dressed (Matt. 22: 1–14). Why should there be this hypersensitivity about invitations? Even more strange, why do some people put up with a rude and bored Mongrober as their guest? At first it seems that the God of the New Testament is all on the side of the worried host whose guests, if they turn up at all, seem not to be joining in the spirit of the occasion: ". . . like unto children sitting in the market-places, who cry out to their playmates and say, We have piped to you and ye have not danced, we have lamented and ye have not mourned" (Matt. 11: 16–17). He seems to be against those who decline to be included in other people's consumption rituals. But his attitude is more complex. He is also against any use of hospitality as a means of exclusion:

When thou givest a dinner or a supper, call not thy friends, or thy brethren, or thy kinsmen, or rich neighbors, lest perchance they likewise invite thee in return, and it serve thee as thy reward. But when thou givest a feast, invite the poor, the crippled, the lame, the blind . . . (Luke 14: 12–14).

Kinship and Marriage

Gospel aside, all that has been cited so far serves to support the idea, so favored by sociologists and economists, that envy and competitiveness are basic to unredeemed human nature. However, there is another kind of society that is not trying to widen and improve its circle of commensality. Trollope portrays it equally well, and on close inspection it is no more lovable than the other. The county families of Herefordshire, repeatedly intermarried, and the great aristocratic families, also intermarried, are not trying to extend their acquaintance. They are closed and stable groups, privileged, holding to their privileges, and jealously guarding their women. The fringe world, competing with names of food and wine, geographical names, and names of guests, are trying to break into the privileged circles, but they cannot synthesize what they know because of lack of historical depth and other gaps and discontinuities in their experience. Though both classes have the same consumption norms, set by the highest incomes, they differ in the economies their poorer members make. Since people have always known each other within the closed classes, external show is unnecessary. Widows and impoverished squires do not disguise their stringencies. But for those attempting to marry up, it is the other way around: Trollope shows them intent on preserving a public show and economizing in private. So in Trollope two different consumption patterns are discerned according to the marriage form: the closed groups practice endogamy as the ideal and use it as a form of closure against outsiders; consumption habits, deemed natural as skin, are criteria for membership and become weapons of exclusion. The other pattern, seeking to marry upwards as the ideal, uses consumption finesse as a technique of usurpation. Since earning potential depends on marriage much more dramatically than it does on other ways of self-advancement, Trollope's society displays a dual marriage pattern that in some essentials and for similar reasons corresponds to the model of certain Southern Bantu-speaking tribes.[15] Among the Tswana, Kgatla, Shona, Venda, and others, the political system is such that everyone is well advised to marry as close to power as possible. That single maxim is enough to explain why the top elite likes to marry into its own circle, while everyone else likes to make a marriage that will link them by ties of close kinship into that circle. Of course marriage and earning potential do not always go together. But when the first governs the second, and when there are big discrepancies in income levels, the pressures result in a combination of marrying-up and marrying-in strategies that connect the flow of goods and of marriages in a regular fashion.

No need to read in Trollope or the ethnographic record for this in-marrying tendency of elite women. In table 4–1, the social groups in England are ranked in order of social status and income expectations; the proportion of men marrying wives from different social groups is also shown.

TABLE 4-1

Degree of Assortive Mating in Britain in 1949

		Percentage Marrying Wives from Social Group			
Social Group of Husbands		I	II	III	IV
I.	Professional and managerial	37	36	21	6
II.	Supervisory and other nonmanual	6	34	41	18
III.	Skilled manual	3	20	54	24
IV.	Unskilled and semi-skilled	1	15	43	41
	All groups	6	24	46	25

NOTE: Reprinted by permission of the publisher from *Social Mobility in Britain* by David Glass, (London: Routledge & Kegan Paul, 1966), p. 331. © 1966 by Routledge & Kegan Paul.

This is an extraordinarily interesting table. In its own terms it shows that 73 percent of the men of the top class marry women who are either from their own social class or from the adjacent class below them. At first glance it looks like a straightforward case of men being willing to marry down and women being willing to marry up, "hypergamy," in anthropological terms. If the normal pattern of this behavior which is found in the ethnographic record holds, the women who make the upward movement will generally be rather well endowed with nonhuman capital. But what about the women in the top social class? Being already at the top, they cannot marry higher, and since their own menfolk are taking wives from outside their class, they have the problem of finding a husband without marrying down. Looking at the table, we do not see a parallel tendency for these high class women to choose husbands in the other classes: only 6 percent of the wives of class II come from class I; only 3 percent for class III, and 1 percent for class IV. The same source, David Glass's survey, gives further confirmation. The higher the social class, the smaller the proportion of "ever-married" (i.e., married, widowed, or divorced) women of the 40–49 age-group. There is no noticeable trend in the proportions of ever-married men in different social groups. But for women the proportions of ever-married increase consistently with decreasing status. The difference between the highest and the lowest social group is around 10 percent.[16]

The problem of finding dowries and settlements or otherwise arranging for the marriages of upper class women is worldwide. Often it is solved by reducing their numbers by female infanticide, or by letting rich men take several wives—polygyny, or both. In our own society, in default of such solutions, these women either marry at a later age or never marry at all if they do not triumph in the fierce competition for eligible husbands. No need to read Victorian novels to recognize what this implies for the competitive raising of consumption standards. And it is quite mistaken to sneer at boy-meets-girl themes in popular literature and film: beating the social barriers is not a trivial but a major matter of concern to all who find themselves excluded.

Lévi-Strauss [17] distinguished among three communication systems constituting social life: the communication of goods, the communication of women, and the communication of words. Though he has put out various suggestions about how they might be related, he has never succeeded in synthesizing a general theory of kinship and mythology on their own. The argument here is that they can never be synthesized without becoming part of a theory of consumption. The meanings conveyed along the goods channel are part and parcel of the meanings in the kinship and mythology channels, and all three are part of the general concern to control information. Only when they are scanned together will they yield their meanings to cultural anthropology.

Sharing goods and being made welcome to the hospitable table and to the marriage bed are the first, closest fields of inclusion, where exclusion operates spontaneously long before political boundaries are at stake. In the structure of a culture consumption, commensality, and cohabitation are forms of sharing; degrees of admission to each are often depicted by analogy with one another. Studies of the ancient Israelites,[18] contemporary Thai villagers,[19] and contemporary Lele tribesmen in the Congo show how their world is organized in a recursive system of metaphors dealing with admission to bed, board, and cult.[20] No one likes to recognize that the capacity to share all three is socially endowed, a result of current decisions, and not an ineluctable fact of nature. Instead, whenever exclusion is operated to define a category of outsiders, the segregated category tends to be credited with a different nature, due to a primeval covenant with God, a present phase in the transmigration of souls, or as in the Lele case, a divine calling made manifest by procreative achievements.

By such categorizing, shared culture is transformed into shared nature. The glove comes to fit like a skin, and anyone who has not the required credentials has a hard task to break in. "When one man is a peer and another a ploughman, that is an accident. One doesn't find fault with the ploughman, but one doesn't ask him to dinner," says Mr. Wharton, Queen's

Council, whose brother is heir to one of Trollope's Herefordshire family estates. Consistently, he adds: "Some people, of whom I confess I am one, consider that like should marry like," and again, to his daughter: "One is bound to be very careful. How can I give you to a man I know nothing about? An adventurer? What would they say in Herefordshire?" To which she replies, "I don't know why they should say anything, but if they did I shouldn't much care," words that she has bitter grounds for retracting as the story of *The Prime Minister* goes on.

We have cast our argument about goods in terms of access to information. Those who can control that access act rationally if they seek a monopoly advantage. Their rational strategy then would be to erect barriers against entry, to consolidate control of opportunities, and to use techniques of exclusion. For those excluded, the only two strategies are to withdraw and consolidate around the remaining opportunities, or to seek to infiltrate the monopolistic barrier. Since consumption is a field in which exclusion can be applied, usurpation attempted, or withdrawal enforced by private individuals against one another, an anthropological theory of consumption must deal with these strategies. But so far any attempts to interpret the demand for goods which ignore these preoccupations about reaching or conserving power and privilege can only fall back upon consumer irrationality. Theories of consumption which assume a puppet consumer, prey to the advertiser's wiles, or consumers jealously competing for no sane motive, or lemming consumers rushing to disaster, are frivolous, even dangerous. Such irrational explanations of consumer behavior get currency only because economists believe that they should have a theory that is morally neutral and empty of judgment, whereas no serious consumption theory can avoid the responsibility of social criticism. Ultimately, consumption is about power, but power is held and exercised in many different ways. A theory of consumption should be a focused beam of light on social policy.

We seem here to be moving with the tide, for a recent Royal Commission on the Distribution of Income and Wealth states that

Income is a means of access to a social system. The significance of low income is that it restricts such access. Below a certain level it may virtually exclude people from participating fully in the life of the community of which they are members. In relation to that community they may then be said to be in poverty.[21]

Social Conditions for Rational Behavior

A stray thread needs to be stitched back into the argument here. We have shown that consumption is used as a method of exclusion from control, but we have not shown why such exclusion is likely to inhibit a rational interpretation of the universe. By the end of this essay we hope to show that the higher families are in the social hierarchy, the more closely involved they are likely to be with each other, and in a much wider social network than the bottom classes. This argument is, of course, contrary to the received idea that the working class household enjoys a richly varied social life on its own street. A very interesting survey of leisure activities in Great Britain shows that the exact opposite is in fact the case. (See table 4–2.)

From every point of view—geographical radius, number of activities, link between work and leisure, not being active members of clubs—the semi-skilled and unskilled class has the shortest range, with the skilled class the next shortest and the professional and managerial class the longest. For example, men's TV-watching hours go up as social class goes down; but active membership of clubs, the average number of leisure activities, the average number of friends seen in the week prior to the survey, and the average number of activities all go up with social class.[22]

TABLE 4-2
Consumption Activities According to Social Class

	Social Class			
Description	AB	C1	C2	DE
Total hours worked	2697	2477	2526	2503
Hours on journey to work	6.1	5.6	4.1	3.5
Average hours worked	48.2	44.7	47.8	47.6
Avg. no. activities*				
Home based	5.7	5.9	5.2	4.2
Active & sports	5.0	4.4	3.9	3.1
TV-watching: hrs. — men	10.0	12.8	12.9	13.3
Some link between work				
& leisure (Percent)	39	12	22	8
Not active members of				
clubs (Percent)	31	49	51	64
Avg. no. leisure activities				
Car owner	18.8	17.1	15.7	13.8
No car	14.1	13.2	12.6	10.3
Avg. no. friends seen in				
previous week	13.6	7.4	10.2	10.8

*Max. = 50.

NOTE: Reprinted by permission of the publisher from *The Symmetrical Family: A Study of Work and Leisure in the London Region*, by Michael Young and Peter Willmott, (London: Routledge and Kegan Paul, 1973). © 1973 by Routledge and Kegan Paul.

But even if the social life of the street were as rich as the nostalgic idyll often implies, the homogeneous working class social environment is never going to provide the sort of information that the middle class family can get by its social contacts. There is another kind of information which some can scan and contribute to, making some things relevant by the mere act of harkening, and other things irrelevant by ignoring them. To be in control of this sort of information may be vital for getting and keeping a high earning potential. To be outside its range altogether, for the individual who can neither hear it nor make his voice heard, is to risk being treated like a stone, trodden underfoot and kicked aside—a limit to future choosing and to the exercise of rational choice.

This sounds farfetched and exaggerated. But it bears directly on the meaning of Rowntree's term, "secondary poverty," where "earnings would be sufficient for the maintenance of merely physical efficiency were it not that some portion of it is absorbed by other expenditure, either useful or wasteful." [13] What is the right procedure for a person who finds himself in a dead end? Some situations isolate the individual from opportunity: there are dead-end jobs and backwater neighborhoods. More than likely a man's chance of not being made redundant in the next decade, and certainly his ability to guide his children into the mainstream, depend on the scale of consumption he maintains. He should stay on good terms with his father's friends and his old work-mates, and keep in touch with his brothers and sisters and nephews and nieces. Earning often depends on wide-flung sources of information which can only be reached through shared consumption. One way to keep off the slide from temporary unemployment to unemployability, which leads to chronic isolation, deviance for his children, even criminality, is to be more closely involved with people. And this takes money.

As elsewhere in this essay, the comparison with rich and poor at the international level is the most illuminating way of making the point. I turn here to Aaron Wildavsky's comparison of budgeting conditions in different countries:

Except in a period of total stagnation we live in an uncertain world. Uncertainties stem from a variety of causes. It is often difficult even to find out exactly what has happened in the past year and to evaluate it or assess the value of the information received (even if it is forthcoming). Often, knowledge of current processes is even more sketchy, so that a valid basis for prediction is by no means assured.

Add to this the problems connected with costing future activities—in conditions where prices cannot be accurately estimated, and in new activities whose costs are unknown—and it seems clear that effective budgeting must find some way of compensating for the lack of omniscience.

This is in fact what happens in countries with effective budgeting processes. These countries enjoy enough surplus resources to allow for mistakes—under- and overestimating, and taking risks without disastrous consequences. This is the essence of being rich. . . . In terms of budgeting, the redundancy enjoyed by rich countries is crucial. Particularly during innovation whether technical, policy, or organizational—redundancy compensates for uncertainty. In place of economy and rationalization, the budget system incorporates duplication, competition, and back-up systems. Instead of attempting comprehensiveness and maximum accountability, it relies on cross checks, continuous feedback, and trust. It stresses reliability instead of, and sometimes at the cost of, efficiency. . . . In areas of uncertainty, particularly those of continuous innovation, elements of redundancy are called into play to offset lack of knowledge, complexity, unknown costs, and unforeseen events. The ability to do this calls for resources—and not merely financial resources—over and above the exact amount which turn out to have been needed for the purpose." [24]

Wildavsky then goes on to develop the contrast between rich and poor countries. The poor face more uncertainties, and their decisions matter more; the effects of one source of uncertainty ramify upon the rest, internal and external. His whole account of the forms of budgeting adopted to deal with grave uncertainties and poor resources is a model of how we should be thinking of the behavior of poor individuals. And above all, his analysis of how initial failure to control the uncertainties rebounds on all decisions should be well digested by anyone who tries to understand the multiple effects of poverty on rational economic behavior. [25]

The upshot is that exclusion from the club of the rich may mean that there is no way of ordering a rational experience at a more modest level in the same universe. For the rich who call the tune are continually changing it, too. The price of order and rationality for those who are neither rich, nor in control, nor in a position to challenge control, is to withdraw.[26] Only in some appropriately poor, and permanently poor, perspective, can they set their valuations on themselves and create the conditions of limited economic rationality. Irrational in the eyes of the privileged, often the refusal of the poor to enter their children in the race for higher education is based on an accurate view of the probable outcome. French surveys have shown how well working class mothers can assess the probability of their children's education leading to better economic opportunities.[27] A self-validating prediction, of course, but not irrational.

Chapter 5

THE TECHNOLOGY
OF CONSUMPTION

Composite Commodities

Man is a social being. We can never explain demand by looking
only at the physical properties of goods. Man needs goods for
communicating with others and for making sense of what is
going on around him. The two needs are but one, for communication can only be formed in a structured system of meanings.
His overriding objective as a consumer, put at its most general,
is a concern for information about the changing cultural scene.
That sounds innocent enough, but it cannot stop at a concern
merely to get information; there has to be a concern to control
it. If he is not in any position of control, other people can
tamper with the switchboard, he will miss his cues, and meaning will be swamped by noise. So his objective as a rational
consumer also involves an effort to be near the center of transmission and an effort to seal off the boundaries of the system.
Being near the center requires a strategy of organizing the exchange of marking services so as not to be excluded from shared
civilities, from neither drinks, nor board, nor the possible
matrimonial bed.

So here we are, with an interpretation of consumer behavior that lines us all up together, us with our machine-made merchandise and the tribesmen with their home-bred flocks and herds and hand-hafted hoes and hand-woven baskets. But it promises nothing of value unless it can improve the economist's computations. He is a professional with a job to do.

The more anxiously we urged on economists this idea of why people really want goods, the more we came to realize that economists are very busy people. Their own professional bias is neither politically inspired nor haphazard, but grounded instead in a powerful technology of measurement and calculation. It will serve no purpose to skate on the surface of their work. If there is to be any useful insight from anthropology for the theory of consumption, the eager anthropologist has to plunge into the trap-bestrewed forest, the most recondite area of demand theory, and try to see if any of the problems which interest economists there is likely to yield to a new approach.

In the end, after threshing around hopefully, the theoretical fields that seemed most susceptible were those in which economists try to interpret major consumption trends, and in which they seek ways of combining goods into large composite classes that respond in the same way to changes in income and prices. Food is the clearest example of a composite commodity. It includes all kinds of drinks, appetizers, staples, and garnishing, yet something meaningful can be said about the average cost of or demand for food. To assume that there are in real life other big partitions between goods fits well the intuition that people do first allocate their expenditures broadly between categories and then, at later stages of decision and choice, make subdivisions within these categories. For instance, having chosen a house in a certain neighborhood, of a certain size, I have committed myself to heating and flooring of some kind, but later comes the choice of possible types of heating and of carpets or tiles. But the distance of the house from my place of work and its selection implies a set of interdependent decisions about transport. It would be extremely convenient and helpful to economists to know more about the basis on which those practical groupings are habitually made by individual consumers. However, the ramifications are so closely meshed and interdependent that it is hard to find an overall principle of grouping goods that will actually simplify their estimates. What makes it particularly difficult is the weakness of economists' assumptions about why people want goods. So it is here, by introducing the social dimension of needs, that anthropology may be able to help. If goods fall into large separable groupings such that "marginal rates of substitution for certain pairs of commodities are functionally independent of the quantities of certain other commodities," [1] then it must be because certain consumption activities can be clumped together and separated out from others. We take consumption activities to be always social activities. It would seem then that the clue to finding real partitioning among goods must be to trace some underlying partitioning in society.

By far the most common of the attempts at grouping goods is the Engel curve, which separates necessities from luxuries according to income elasticity. [2] Necessities are defined as those goods which are bought in the same quantities regardless of changes in prices or incomes. So needful are they to the consumer's way of life that when his income falls, he still buys much the same amount. Food is the class of goods on which the poor spend a larger part of their income than the rich. This proportion holds good so widely over the world (with some adaptations in the mode of calculation) that it is known as Engel's law. Food as a composite commodity is also the prime necessity. Luxuries, by contrast, are a completely heterogeneous class defined as those goods on which the individual will quickly cut down, in response to a drop in income. The distinction is culturally neutral and purely technical. That it happens to slot neatly into the veterinary prejudice (that food is what the poor most want) has perhaps been seen as an added advantage of the analysis. Also implied is the idea that expenditure on luxuries is slightly immoral. This is ever-tempting but misleading, as we shall see. Part of our task will be to restore the neutrality of luxuries in the eyes and hearts of economists.

New Commodities

An interesting and central problem is how to spot a new necessity in advance of the signal from price movements and ownership levels. Goods arrive in the shops today: some of them will become tomorrow's necessities. What is the direction and power that selects among the modern luxuries and procures that shift in status, so that from being first unknown, then known but dispensable, some goods become indispensable?

"Twenty years ago I had no car, no television, no refrigerator, no washing machine and no garden, how in heaven's name could I have been happy then?" [3] In their turn each of these things came in as new commodities—all except the garden; in turn (including the garden), demand for them has spread right through the population, or almost. The curve that started to show a slow demand quickened and steepened, and then gradually flattened off, so that over time it shows the S-shaped form which generally characterizes new commodities. The flat head of the S shows saturation, the point where few new markets are being opened up. The main sales are for replacements and improved versions. At this point the market is defined as saturated. It may be saturated at any level of possible ownership, whether it is 90 percent or 30 percent of households, when demand turns downward. The economist can assume that all who want the thing have now got it. That saturation can set in long before even the 70 percent of households are equipped poses no special problem. Tastes and habits are not within the technical competence of economists; they are content to leave them to anthropologists. But surely we must be interested in asking why demand for some goods slackens off somewhere very short of complete acceptance, while for others it rushes on until 80 percent of households count it as basic equipment. The question is what makes yesterday's luxuries turn into today's necessities—not forgetting that some of yesterday's luxuries have dropped out completely. For instance, consider the solid silver cigarette cases of forty to fifty years ago, which, no longer carried, have not yet joined the display of Georgian snuffboxes in the curiosity cabinet, but lie instead stacked in attics, awaiting a decision as to their value—antiques or just their weight in silver.

Regarding the long term, the economist seems to have no answer. For the short term, the answer is in terms of prices and incomes, within the theory of demand. But the theory expects that a buoyant demand will make it worthwhile for suppliers to search for ways of lowering their costs of production: prices will eventually come down to an acceptable level, or credit facilities will help to bridge the consumer's financing problem.

To consider saturation from an anthropological perspective, we will keep in view the history of two innovations that have entered our homes in the past century: one is a universally agreed necessity, the television set; while the other, the telephone, is a necessity in upper class homes. In England, for example, this innovation has not penetrated to all the potential users. In 1948 the percentage of households owning television sets was 0.3 percent. By 1958 it was 52 percent, while the telephone, introduced in 1877, by the same date was installed in only 16.5 percent of households. Dividing the distribution according to social class, the television is very evenly spread, contrasting with the telephone, which clusters thickly at the top.

Two years later the proportion of all households owning television sets had gone up to 65 percent. By contrast, telephone penetration had actually reached no further than 21.4 percent by 1965. By 1973 there had been some catching up. The penetration rates for television were about 90 percent in all social classes, and for the telephone they were about 45 percent overall, with 88 percent in class A,B; 67 percent in C1; 44 percent in C2; and 20 percent in D,E.

Since TV and telephone are both relatively new means of communication, it will be instructive to compare their paths. Economists' usual practice is to treat television as one more household durable. The *National Institute of Economic and Social Research Review,* from which the figures are drawn, compared television sets with refrigerators, washing machines, and vacuum cleaners. Graham Pyatt improved on this by selecting two sets of durables, one, a kitchen set consisting of cooker, vacuum cleaner, washing machine, and refrigerator, and the other apparently an entertainment set, radio, record player, radiograph, and television,[4] but he ignored the telephone. Lancaster tried grouping all goods—including men's clothing, auto-

TABLE 5-1

*Distribution of Television and
Telephone Services, 1958*

Class	Television Sets Ownership*	Telephone Installation†
Upper (A, B)	57.3%	67.8%
Middle (C1)	53.4	25.3
Lower (C2, D, E)	51.1	5.0

*"The Demand for Domestic Appliances," *National Institute of Economists Review*, p. 21, 1960, data from p. 27, Table 2, The Social Pattern of Ownership.

†Courtesy of the Post Office, Central Headquarters, Statistics, and Business Research Department, "Forecasting of Residential Telephone Penetration by Use of the Techniques of Social Sectors, Revised estimates."

mobiles, vegetables—on the basis of their intrinsic properties,[5] but he does not mention telephones. The whole problem of choosing a relevant grouping for the sake of comparisons of consumer behavior is like a corpse-strewn battlefield, and usually too technical for an outsider to comment upon.[6] We hope, however, to show that an anthropological understanding of the consumer's objectives will afford new ways of grouping. Unfortunately, there has been no close comparative study of the rates of advance of television and the telephone in the United Kingdom. Nevertheless, as one has had a meteoric spread, while the other has advanced slowly, it is interesting to use the comparison as a testing ground of the current theories of economists.

Spread-of-Infection Model

The spread of television is a good illustration of the infectious disease model, or the epidemiological model of the spread of innovation. Each household as it acquires a set becomes itself, as it were, immune, but its presence is likely to infect other households with the bug. People usually buy what they see their friends using and enjoying. Social contacts are not random. The likelihood of a TV owner influencing anyone he never meets is low. Each member of the population who becomes an owner reduces the number of susceptible nonowners in a circle of friends. So the rate of spread is affected by any discontinuities, regional and social, in personal relationships. Bain found that the rate of spread of TV was influenced by the size of families: the smaller families could afford the opportunity sooner than the larger ones, a smaller family being, in this argument, equivalent to a higher per capita income for the household.[7] Apart from this, the rate of spread of TV between different classes depended on the numbers in each social class: the more numerous, the slower the rise in proportion of ownership. It took twice as long to reach 50 percent in class D as in class A, one and a half times as long as in class B, and one and a quarter times as long as in class C. He showed that the main process that slows up the spread of ownership is the equivalent of immunity against disease. In the end, everyone has had it once and the population is then immune. For future sales, unless the population expands, the interest focuses on replacement of existing TV sets, or, by means of improvements, convincing owners that their set is obsolete, or that they now need two kinds, or perhaps one of the same kind for each member of the family. The epidemiological model fits perfectly the case of television spread. But it says nothing to help us understand the nonspread of telephones in the same period.

Purely economic reasons (in terms of the high initial cost of installing a telephone) do not take us far. If the price of subscribing to a telephone was too high, a steady demand would have eventually brought it down. By 1959 all four appliances studied in the *NIESR Review* (1960) were being sold at relative prices far below what they had been in the consumer prices index of 1959. Evidently, the principle of immunity itself needs to be examined. Indeed, the comparison of a new commodity with a diagnosable, nameable disease is misleading, because each commodity is linked to others whose relations as complements and substitutes should be scanned altogether. We must move away from considering each commodity separately towards considering a particular level of technology that sustains a community at a given place and time.

Several economists have recognized that in the long term, prices, being responses to demand, can hardly be used as explanations of demand. Only the most short-term and superficial effects can be explained by price changes, and even by incomes. Trying to analyze changes in the demand for tea, beer, spirits, and tobacco in the 1870–1958 period (omitting the war years), Prest concluded that price and income explained 1 percent of the variance of consumption of tea and tobacco, 9 percent of spirits, and 17.5 percent of beer.[8] Commenting upon this exercise, Farrell agrees that the strictly economic variables were quite unimportant in determining demand. In the long run social variables, which he put together as time trends and discontinuities, swamped price and income effects.[9] This reads like another invitation to the less exact social sciences to come into the discussion. Ironmonger takes up the theme even more emphatically.[10] He divides commodities between those remaining steady, those starting on the upward demand trend, and those having dropped out of fashion in the period between 1920 and 1938. They can be called the established, the inmoding, and the outmoded. The outmoded commodities in this important exercise turned out to be dried fruits and legumes, once luxuries, flour and cocoa, once necessities, but gradually going downward in importance. Something was happening to the shopping lists during those 19 years which does not yield its secret to the straight inspection of prices and incomes. Like Prest and Farrell, Ironmonger is ready to concede some non-economic factors, and, following Bain, he elaborates the infection model of spread of innovation to trace them. But this model focuses on the rate of change in the upward swing of demand and leaves a clutter of mysteries at the slowing down phase, where tastes are invoked to explain why everyone who has not got the thing does not want to have it.

What were those tastes? Twenty years earlier than 1938 was another culture with another technology base. As far as marking services were concerned, we need to be able to show how changes in the technological base (defined by consumption activities), due to increasing industrialization, affect the scale of activities open to people and the means by which they are pursued. For example, the outmoded commodities, dried fruits, legumes, cocoa, and flour, meant the joys of sharing rich hot puddings, some with outrageous names—spotted Dick, baby's leg, jam rolypoly, as well as prune mold, chocolate shape, rich soggy suet puddings, pease pudding, and so on. All those things themselves were only items in an exchange of marking services. We need to get closer to the conditions for getting and giving marking services to be able to analyze changing tastes in economic terms.

Order of Acquisition

Industrialization has complicated life for the consumer. Regarding material goods there are, indeed, more of many things. But to keep up with the exchange of marking services necessary to happiness and necessary to a coherent, intelligible culture, he has to run harder to keep in the same place. Industrial growth means nothing more or less than extending the scale of operations. This is how per capita product is increased. The division of labor, as Adam Smith saw, inexorably drives producers to find economies of scale, and this drives them to finer and finer differentiation of their product and to search for wider markets. Large-scale plants need a dense population to supply labor, hence the shift of rural populations into cities. Life in a city entails higher costs of sanitation, water supply, and so on, and new costs in transporting, distributing, packaging, and preserving food. New trades and professions arise, themselves calling for new kinds of goods. Responding to the change in the structure of society, the household transfers its production processes to the market, and buys more and more of its goods there with the money it has earned. No wonder canned foods have taken the place of home-bottling, and no wonder home deep-freezers are competing with canned foods. The household, like the manufacturer, seeks economies of scale in time and energy in its productive processes.

Some idea of efficient consumption could be worked out if

the technology would only stay fixed. One would take into account the social demands for expenditure at various stages in the life cycle and allow for size of households and age of members. One would be able to say roughly that a youth requires the wherewithal to find a wife, that a married couple needs a home of some sort, that needs will expand with the birth of children and contract with old age and retirement. This is very much what the anthropologist does to describe the economy of a tribe at a given time. Among the pastoral Turkana the average head of household needed to deploy his family as herdsmen and dairymaids over 100 to 150 head of small livestock (sheep and goats), 25 to 30 head of cattle, and a few camels and donkeys. These quantities would cover the daily subsistence of humans, the replacement of flocks and herds, and also the contingencies of debt, loans to friends, bad years, and so on. A few rich men held up to 100 cattle and over 300 small stock. A very few paupers eked out existence on wild fruits and occasional labor for wealthier people.[11] The average Lele man in the Congo would have to reckon on spending 300 to 400 raffia cloths, plus camwood bars, axes, and hoes, for admission fees, fines, and gifts before he had established his first wife's family.[12] If, for some reason (such as the early death of his own father), he were not able to raise the right amounts of goods at the critical time, he would be forced to pawn one of his sisters and suffer a severe diminution of his civil rights.

The task of assessing needs in real terms is much more complicated if the basic technology is changing rapidly, as in the modern industrial world. However, the changes are always in roughly the same direction, toward more industrialization, more specialization in the division of labor. Consequently, it ought to be possible to work out the shifting technological basis of consumption at least in respect of essentials, and to use the levels of ownership of major pieces of equipment as a measure of standard of living.

Paroush has set out to do just this. Indeed, he finds that the order of acquisition of certain key items is roughly the same in all industrial countries.[13] His technique for establishing the common order of acquisition is highly empirical. Surveying the distribution of goods between households, he selects those which 90 percent of all consumers will purchase in the same order. He rigorously limits his work to those goods and excludes all others. His method is explicitly designed to take account of the shifts in needs which arise from demographic changes. There are some consumer durables whose usefulness rises with the size of family, such as the washing machine. A bachelor need not own an oven till he marries, so the order radio-before-oven is likely to hold good, by reason of the social definition of bachelor. But Paroush rules out idiosyncratic needs because no universal order of preference is likely to show for them. For example, he cites the need of an able-bodied individual for crutches, and the need of the unmusical for a piano: a piano "is really essential for a pianist, but a luxury piece of furniture for a music-hater." [14]

Paroush rightly sets great store by the possible applications of his method. The stage of acquisition of a given household, once the general pattern of acquisition is established, can serve as an ordinal index of the standard of living, and changes in the standard of living can be traced by noting percentages of ownership of certain goods. The household's commodity composition being the result of past income, and influenced by expectation of future income, should provide a good index of normal income. Obviously, the method could lend itself to many interesting analyses. Dividing the population of Israel into income levels, and examining the distribution of families by income within each level, he finds "a conspicuous correlation between income and ownership from the poorest through to the richest level. For every level of outlay, the percentage of families with less than the given outlay declines as the level becomes richer." But the conclusion he draws is premature: "As a by-product we get a natural definition of the

relative essentiality of various goods." Since the levels of ownership are measured within defined income levels, his method, as
it stands, can only say how much an individual household devi-
ates from the commodity composition deemed essential in
its income group. Unless he boldly plumps for an arbitrary
level of ownership which every household in this day and age
should reach to be competent in current technological performance, he cannot talk about essentiality except for a given
class of incomes.

There are two snags about his assumptions. First, the concept of efficiency is tied to the normal performance of each
income group. This puts him in good company, as it is the same
snag that besets utility theory in general. Second, his method
necessarily selects the goods which lend themselves to grouping in a strict scale structure. Any goods on which tastes dis-
agree systematically will escape through the meshes of his net.
This means that he can never use it to capture the existence of
two or more distinct technologies of consumption in the same
economy. These shortcomings could be repaired. Some combination of this method with Graham Pyatt's technique for
assessing the probability of owning a particular set of goods
could be devised to ferret out the different patterns. In the survey that Pyatt analyzed, "highly significant differences were
found between the estimated probability patterns for different
social classes." [15] This being so, the task of giving a technological basis to the idea of essentiality or necessity must not
be shirked, though it may have to take a different turn.

Paroush's comment on music-haters is misleading and in-
consistent. It implies a practical, technological basis for the order of acquisition, which is belied by his discovery that radio,
record player, and transistor are more essential for bachelors
than are ovens. Even if he insists that the radio and transistor
are wanted for tuning in to useful information, surely the record player at least suggests a priority for the wish for music.
For how is the bachelor ever going to get married unless he has

Drawn by ye Author — Etch'd by J.ᵒ Gilray

CORBIE FARM 1782

MODERN MONEY
Betty's Money

Enough for a Mansion
Betty, spin and
& their Freehold

Farmer Giles & his Wife shewing off their daughter Betty
to their Neighbours on her return from School

introduced by the January College by H. Humphrey &

FIGURE 5-1

Farmer Giles and His Wife Put Their Daughter Through Her Paces for a Prospective Husband

Drawing by James Gillray (1809). Original in the Mansell Collection. Reprinted by Permission.

some social accomplishments? Graham Pyatt speaks more realistically to the anthropological ear when he remarks that the trend to diffusion of durables, which may be described as a change of tastes, would be more fully understood as learning: "the implications of genuine technological development are the same as those of a learning process." [16] Some people are born musical and others can try to learn music, but the learning may well be held to be very necessary. In Gilray's cruel caricature, "Farmer Giles and his wife put their daughter through her paces for a prospective husband." [17] Evidently the girl had to play the piano or be condemned to a lowly marriage and poorer home. After the Rotterdam bombings in 1940 and 1941, middle and upper class families used household inventories for claiming compensation from the government. At that time, refrigerators, washing machines, and water heaters were comparatively recent innovations, and ownership of these appliances was rare and restricted to the highest income groups. But for all the rest, the ownership frequency and saturation levels showed upon the Rotterdam inventories as follows:[18]

TABLE 5-2
The Rotterdam Inventories

	Saturation Level
Vacuum cleaner	100%
Sewing machine	90
Piano	85

Evidently learning the piano was a necessary accomplishment for Dutch boys and girls of a certain social class.

Paroush writes as if efficiency were a matter of keeping up with the advanced technology of speed and physical comfort. He refers to up-market goods such as air conditioners, and he fully realizes that his technique ought to explain something about the up-market concept. But unless he can take marking services and the culturally standardized norms of social interaction into account, he is limited arbitrarily to those few goods which can be scaled by 90 percent agreement in their ordering.

Personal Availability

Too much open-mindedness and gentility about the possible reasons for choosing goods, and too much delicacy and embarrassment at the idea that human beings might need to keep level with each other so as to be able to enjoy perfect reciprocity—this is the main reproach against economists who have done the most thinking about consumption. Kelvin Lancaster, for example, produces a finely tuned engine for analyzing consumer choice, and he knows that in the last resort it can apply even to the choice of lighting and food at dinner tables.[19] But his total open-mindedness and lack of preconception about the objectives of shared consumption are his undoing. He starts by deploring the fact that traditional demand theory has ignored the properties of the goods themselves:

. . . with no theory of how the properties of goods affect preferences at the beginning, traditional analysis can provide no predictions as to how demand would be affected by a specified change in one or more properties of a good, or how a "new" good would fit into the preference pattern over existing goods. Any change in any property of any good implies that we have a new preference pattern for every individual: we must throw away any information derived from observing behaviour in the previous situation and begin again from scratch. . . .[20]

Lancaster directs attention to the agreed physical properties of goods and their uses, whether social or psychological or nutritional. He argues that individuals are more interested in the characteristics of goods than in the goods themselves. When they choose, they are showing direct preferences for particular collections of characteristics and the preference for the actual goods that carry them is derived or indirect. His project for providing a fully integrated theory of consumer demand starts with an attempt to separate those properties of demand which are universal and depend on agreed characteristics that supply universal wants, and those which depend only on the idiosyncratic preferences of individuals. His exercise is made unduly cumbersome by the inability to conceive systematically of the consumer as a social being. Consequently, when he thinks of universal needs he is driven back to universal physical needs. His examples are drawn from automobile performance, speed, comfort, noise, or from calories and proteins as the needed properties in food which underlie the demand for food. The materialist approach to human needs works well enough for the limited purposes to which his theory has been applied. But a more consistently sociological approach would give it added power and the promise of a really strong theory of the technology of consumption. As it is, Lancaster is no more able than anyone else to explain which properties of today's luxuries will make some of them, but not others, become tomorrow's necessities.

To get a theoretical grip on the relationship between technology and consumption, it is no good starting with an unbiased mind as to what physical properties of goods are relevant, nor will enlightenment come by devising an analytical tool that can deal with all possible appreciations of all possible physical properties in all possible consumer activities. Some simplifying assumptions are needed. As far as anthropology is concerned, there is only one type of physical property of consumption goods that need be considered: the capacity of goods to increase personal availability.

The demand for marking services implies a demand for personal availability. Sending a telegram to be read out at a friend's wedding is not the same quality of service as traveling a thousand miles to be there. Sending flowers by telegraph to a friend in the hospital is not the same quality of personal service as arriving in person at the usual visiting hours. But however willing, one cannot attend two friends' consumption rituals in person at close intervals of time in two distant places unless travel can be speeded up. Nor can a household increase the number of friends attending its own consumption rituals without increasing the power for dealing with large quantities. More space is needed, more relief from time-consuming household processes. Other things being equal, our theory supposes that a rise in real income will tend to be accompanied by an increase in the frequency of large-scale private social events. The rise in real income will be signaled by a demand for equipment and services which release individuals from a chain of high-frequency tasks in household production. An anthropological definition allows of two kinds of luxuries—one, the mere rank signifiers, such as the best china for the family christening; the other, the newest technological aids, the innovating capital equipment, which relieve the pressure on available time, space, and energy. They remain luxuries until they have become part of the normal technological base from which all consumption activities proceed. Though we cannot tell which new scale-facilitating equipment will slot into the existing cost structure and gradually transform it, we can be fairly sure that rising, real income is expressed as a demand for household scale facilitators.

Surely, one would expect the telephone to have been one of these as soon as it appeared on the market. One would have expected it to quickly become part of the technology base, as it did in the United States and as electric lighting has now done in the United Kingdom. But it did not. What does the epidemiological model say about the slow spread of the telephone in England? That there must have been some principle of immunity to the infection, other than the immunity which comes from acquisition, is an empty answer. We have to seek that *cordon sanitaire* in the status system and in the way that the distribution of status interlocks with the technology of consumption. A possible approach is given in the next chapter, where status is related to personal availability, and the latter to the use of goods implying "scale" of consumption.

Chapter 6

CONSUMPTION PERIODICITIES

Ranking Consumption Events

Legislation can deliberately tax the rich and provide assistance for the poor, and the rich may assent to the redistribution. But if there is an unintended process by which important technical innovations generate advantages that accrue to the already advantaged, it should be important for social policy to identify that process. Since there is little legislation for consumption, and since it is supposed to be an area of free and unconstrained choice, it will be difficult, unless by anthropological comparisons, to identify any simple social mechanism that harnesses consumption to social exclusion. The argument will develop along the following lines.

First, it will be argued that any given state of technology and production can be characterized by a particular pattern of consumption periodicities. (The concept of consumption periodicities will need to be explained.) Then we will indicate the broad correlation that holds between consumption periodicities and rank, high frequency and low rank tending to go in a certain pattern together. Then, arguing a direct relationship be-

tween technology mediated by a pattern of consumption periodicities and access to marking services, we will be able to
return to the view of consumption as a system for the exchange and control of information. On this view, those with
comparative disadvantages in the technology of consumption
will be cumulatively losing out in the struggle to keep information under control. It seems probable that a spontaneous and
apparently unregulated social mechanism sets up the status
barriers which account for differences in consumption patterns.

Start with an imaginary, stable society in which the same set
of marking services is available to all members on universal
criteria of sex, age, married status, and parenthood. An example might be the Tallensi as they described themselves to Meyer
Fortes in the 1940s.[1] A boy is not a man, but he can expect
to be one; a married man can expect to be a father; and a
girl expects to grow to womanhood and be a wife and a mother
and eventually a mother-in-law. For each status, a certain
grade of consumption is judged appropriate; for example, a
man seen carrying a brace of dried guinea fowl can be assumed to be about to present them to his wife's parents. In an
imaginary example nearer home, we would find fairly quickly
that there is a roughly inverse relationship between the frequency of use of objects and the value of the marking services
that they confer. Moreover, the latter normally tends to vary
directly with the number of people present. So it all fits together
neatly. Imagine that each household in this simple, stable culture expects to own one set of glasses, cups, and plates for
every-day use; a best set is kept for Sundays, and a very best
heirloom set is stored on the top shelf wrapped in tissue paper
for annual display at Christmas or New Year's. Thus, the
plates can be used for discriminating between events on a
three-point scale. Much finer discrimination can be signaled
by food, and on a much longer range. Food can discriminate the different times of the day, and one day from another;
as well as the annual events it can also distinguish life-cycle

events such as funerals and weddings. Let us suppose that in this simple culture a parallel gamut is developed for clothing so that every man who finds himself sipping turtle soup and port (life-cycle markers) will inevitably be wearing his lace-frilled shirt and be surrounded by many other men in the same garb. It is easy to suppose that for each higher point on this scale notched by china, food, and clothing, there is an increasing numerical factor for people sharing the event, and increasingly valuable marking services associated with it. We would find that the rank value of each class of goods varies inversely with the frequency of its use: the breakfast is taken separately, more of the family and friends assemble for Sunday dinner, a larger assembly collects for Christmas, and still larger for weddings and funerals. Even in this simple case, when every member of the society has potentially the same scope in his lifetime, the quality differences between goods are markers of the rank of events, as well as the rank of persons. The cultural aspect of necessities is revealed as their service in low-esteem, high-frequency events, while luxuries tend to serve essentially for low-frequency events that are highly esteemed.

Quality

In our experience of goods, periodicity in consumption use marks rank and creates quality goods. Every house normally has beds, but there are beds of different qualities; bread is a necessity for everyone, but because of income elasticities there are luxury breads—and even luxury potatoes. When society is stratified, the luxuries of the common man may become the daily necessities of the upper classes. As between social classes, the periodicity of use does not merely sort out the upper class goods, it also serves to mark differences between classes of people. At the king's court, as it were, it is birthdays and

Christmas every day. Quality is the characteristic of goods that results from their being chosen as rank markers. The following table from the National Food Survey may be suggestive.

TABLE 6-1
*Quality Elasticities**

	Seasonal Prices
Butter	0.01
Cheese	0.03
Sugar	0.03
Fruit	0.03
Eggs	0.04
Bread	0.05
Milk	0.06
Meat	0.07
Fish	0.07
Cakes	0.08
Beverages (tea, coffee)	0.11
Potatoes	0.11
Vegetables	0.16
Cream	0.22

*Quality elasticities are defined as expenditure elasticity minus quantity elasticity.

NOTE: Taken from *Household Food Consumption and Expenditure*, Appendix E, p. 146 (HMSO, 1967).

The quality index measures the difference between expenditure elasticity and quantity elasticity. The table suggests the inverse correlation between frequency and quality that we have been led to expect. Butter is at the bottom of the list, the lowest on the quality index, and presumably, given what we know of our local ethnography and the place of "bread and butter" in our fare, the most frequent, used, say, four times a day, plainly a cultural necessity. Cream, the highest on the quality index, used, say, on Sundays, is a rank marker, a luxury. The only surprise on this list might be potatoes, whose response to seasonal changes in price shows a high regard for quality, but considering the prime place of the potato in the English ceremonial dinner,[2] this only presents confirmation. If there were no new potatoes, and no quality differences between potatoes, they might lose their suitability for main-course, main-meal menus. Before the 1972 rise in prices, the potato producers had cause to worry about the declining place of that vegetable relative to other items of diet. High-quality goods, like lace frills and best china, are pure markers. Usually scarcity keeps quality goods in the steeply sloping curve of income elasticities; quality itself is scarce. A drop in prices would not in itself send potatoes downward to share with dried figs and peas the fate of outmoded commodities, but a dead uniformity of quality which would allow no discriminating between best, good, and ordinary occasions would bring potatoes to the same point in the quality index as bread. One thing we can say, for sure, is that there will always be luxuries, for rank must be marked.

All goods to some extent emanate messages about rank, sets of goods even more so. The class of pure rank-markers could be the high-quality versions that serve no other purpose, like the best porcelain, the family heirlooms, ancestral portraits. But it is not always easy to separate pure rank-marking from practical efficiency. To Marshall Tito, who admired the gold-plated dinner service at Buckingham Palace, Prince Philip confided: "And my wife finds that it saves on breakages." Gold-plated towel rails perhaps tarnish less than chrome, and so save on cleaning time; smoked salmon is light to digest and good for the brain; port soothes the vocal chords. Working our way through the more obvious pure markers, apologetic owners are sure to find some ingenious practical advantage for most of them. However, these are frankly the class of goods of which Professor Myint writes: "In the sphere of luxury products, consumers' demand is certainly very unstable and elusive, 'like streaks of lightning across the sky.' " [3] So let us now say no more about those fashion-ridden luxuries, and concentrate rather on the capacity of goods to facilitate personal availability. Inevitably, such characteristics also mark rank, for ownership levels cannot be disguised. Ownership of scale-facilitating goods indicates social advantage as surely as expenditure on air travel indicates mileage.

Periodicity as a Principle in the Division of Labor

Consider the full effects of this inverse correlation between use frequency and rank or quality. It would be the same, even if everyone were responsible entirely for his own goods, but the principle of the division of labor affords benefits of scale. Consequently, it is good sense to establish a specialized category of persons to whom high-frequency tasks are allotted. Their work is to take charge of those services that are counted as necessities. This will include servicing bodily functions, since the living organism needs daily or more frequent care. Bathroom-cleaning, feeding, bed-making, and care of clothes are rightly counted chores; a chore is essentially nonpostponable, high-frequency. They tend to be ranked as menial tasks, and the goods associated with them, however necessary and intimate, ranked as ordinary stuff, of low value. This association works, even in the very simplest society. So the high-frequency–low-rank correlation becomes a principle of social organization derived from technological factors.

It is good economic sense to use a fixed factor of production to the fullest. Anyone assigned to a high-frequency, nonpostponable task in the household becomes like a fixed factor of production. Consequently, tasks of roughly the same frequency can be allotted to the same person without increasing the marginal costs. Feeding a baby at four-hour intervals can easily be combined with a two-hour schedule for care of a sick person, and other routines can be slotted into the same program. Thus, the division of labor between the sexes is set, the world over, by the best possible economic principles as follows: work frequencies tend to cluster into complementary role categories. These differentiate upward: the higher the status, the less periodicity constraints; the lower the status, the greater the periodicity constraints. In the range of ethnographic illustrations, it is hard to fix a general principle that holds for the division of labor all over the world, apart from the physiological specialization of women for breeding and nursing. Men sometimes cook, spin, weave, and even ply the needle. Women do not usually hunt or go to war, but sometimes they do; they rarely climb trees, but some do. The most general account of the division of labor between the sexes that fits everywhere would be one based on the periodicities of women's work, starting out from the recurring physical services required by small babies, the sick, and the dying. Anyone with influence and status would be a fool to get encumbered with a high-frequency responsibility. Apart from the restrictions on other activity, it is bound to be generally cast as low-status work. In itself high frequency is not incompatible with work that involves covering a large geographical radius, peddling shoelaces or onions, for instance. But if it involves a large radius, such work cannot be combined with other work of compatible frequencies into a composite bundle of household (or national) responsibilities. So the salesman or peddler, however far he travels, is just a salesman or peddler, and the best other function he can take on is bearing gossip. Other high-frequency work fixes a person to a limited radius. But whether localized or geographically dispersed, high-frequency work is not compatible with being available for important tasks of unpredictable occurrence. A big assignment cannot be given to a person who might have to be, in consequence of other responsibilities, in two places at once. So their different frequencies polarize tasks between the more and the less esteemed categories of persons. This is not to say that the single composite role which includes a wide variety of high-frequency work need be bereft of esteem. Any metaphysical scheme worthy of the name and with a spark of imagination can allot complementary forms of esteem to the different roles: a warrior's role is noble, but counterpoised to another different noble role, that of wife and mother. The corporal works of mercy have their religious status; women's role in the domestic sphere has its social backing. But it still remains true that women's work as such puts them outside the areas of decision-making where important information is being generated. Women tend to join the councils of the state only when they can delegate or dodge the periodicity-constrained parts of the normal woman's role.

Between laying the plates on the table four times a day and bringing in the coal once a day, or mowing the lawn once a week, the division of labor in the home follows this pattern. On a national level, too, the laborer's work, when he is in work, is more subject to frequent periodicity constraints than his boss's work. Between households at different income levels, to be poor is to be periodicity-constrained in the processes of household management. The rich housewife's husband has more shirts and she can launder at will, without making him wait after breakfast while she irons a shirt for him to go to work in. If only it was more practicable to use, the measurement of household periodicities would provide an abstractable, objective characteristic of any regular activity. It hints at a technology-based description of poverty. If our urban poor go shopping every day and buy minute quantities of bread, tea, and sugar at each repetitive outing, the hardship is only partly shown in the greater retail costs they incur. Liquidity constraints are compounded by periodicity constraints. There are real technical difficulties in achieving a presence at all-important consumption rituals at which they can hope to enlist help and advice from friends and kin.

According to this thesis, a change in life-styles ought to be recognizable by a change in the pattern of periodicities in household processes. Accordingly, the analysis of periodicities should be a hopeful way to set about identifying the distinction between goods which will enable econometricians to make simpler and yet more accurate estimations. Periodicities give a rough approximation to a major difference in use between necessities and luxuries; future necessities in the present luxuries class will be sets of goods with effective periodicity-relieving properties. A telephone is just such a good, allowing control over the timing or postponement of social events. But most significantly, access to a subculture whose domestic processes are characterized by low-frequency, easily postponable patterns of activity means access to the upper class, wherever that may be. If we could distinguish social categories from each other by understanding the periodicities that govern their use of goods, we would have a tool for grouping classes of goods into broad composite commodities.

Unfortunately, periodicity-analysis, though good for delicate work and motion studies in business and manufacturing, promises to be only a very cumbersome tool for our general purposes..We dwell upon it here not because we expect to engage in it, nor to press anyone else to do so, but because it enables us to establish the technology-based approach to consumption which the later argument will develop.

In our own changing technology, the process of in-moding and outmoding of goods depends, not upon consumer caprice, but upon shifts of the division of labor within and beyond the household, and on the effect of a change in price for one service upon the demand for another. As Gary Becker insists and demonstrates,[4] these are economic matters *par excellence,* and their analysis along orthodox lines dispels the mysteries of consumer tastes and puts the questions about diffusion of new commodities squarely back in the economist's camp. For tastes will evidently change to fit to the general pattern of periodicities synchronizing household production with personal availability at any given level of consumer technology. At the bottom of the social scale, there will be high frequency in the processes of the household, correlated with a small degree of personal availability for joining low-frequency, highly valued consumption events. Moving up the social scale, this trend reverses once inflexible periodicities in the household processes are gradually brought under control. This is what the rise in real income means. Seeking a relationship between periodicities and status is an exercise in structural analysis. It would never have been profitable to look for the meaning or value of goods by taking them individually, item by item. On the analogy of a tune unfolding its pattern in a temporal scheme, the goods reveal their usefulness in the total scheme of periodicities in which they serve. By finding a status relationship that holds between periodicities in use and a scale of consumption rituals, the technology of consumption can be mapped onto socially significant properties. Thus Kelvin Lancaster's approach can acquire sociological content. He need no longer restrict his analytic technique to cars and washing machines, but can extend it to dinner parties, as originally intended.

Now that the understanding of consumption seems to need an analysis of synchronization possibilities, the techniques of time-series analysis in production become applicable.[5] Too powerful a machinery, one might think, for cracking a small nut, but consumption patterns, although extremely elusive, are just as important to track as prices on the stock exchange. The consumer, instead of being regarded as the owner of certain goods, should be seen as operating a pattern of periodicities in consumption behavior, a pattern that can be examined. He is constrained by the number of nonpostponable, high-frequency activities in household production and his availability for consumption rituals can be compared on this basis with that of others. It is similar to a liquidity constraint in its effects on consumption behavior. Perhaps the conception of a periodicities portfolio could be tried. The well-balanced investment portfolio covers its liabilities with an appropriate amount of liquid assets. A household with a consumption portfolio heavily characterized by commitment to high frequency, nonpostponable activities is avoiding risk in a situation in which "a worse than 'expected' outcome must be dreaded more than a better than 'expected' outcome is desired." [6] Hicks said this, arguing that it would be a mistake to consider the liquid part of a balance sheet in isolation. Taking this together with Wildavsky's description of the problems of poverty, in which any worse than expected outcome is disastrous, the advantages of being able to balance the portfolio the other way are equally obvious.

Consuming Level

Consumption periodicities enable us to relate the economists' concept of permanent income to the intelligent realism with which the household deploys its income over marking services. The principle of reciprocity requires exchanges of expenditure on hospitality to match. Matching is therefore very carefully controlled. In the 1930s, *Mass Observation* reported on the habit of drinking level.

All our observations show that the majority of pub-goers tend, when drinking in a group, to drink level: and very often there is not a quarter of an inch difference between the depth of beer in the glasses of a group of drinkers. . . . The greatest lack of uniformity in the rate of drinking in a group is when they are halfway through their glasses; they will all start together, and there is a very strong tendency for them all to finish at once, or nearly simultaneously, at any rate. The simultaneous emptying of glasses is the most frequent form of level drinking.

Even blind people keep in line:

The blind man and three others sit round a table and order pints. As soon as the mugs are brought they lift them to their mouths with a slow "follow through" motion, and keep them there for about four seconds, then put them down simultaneously. All, including the blind man, have drunk about a quarter of the mug, almost level. After this they take smaller gulps, sometimes the blind man starting, sometimes the others; in no special order of beginning or finishing; but gulp for gulp they drink level to within a quarter of an inch throughout.[7]

Keeping to the same level is necessary for the ritual of standing a round of drinks: we can understand it so easily in the microcosm of the pub. Anthropology asks us to consider rituals of reciprocity affecting all kinds of consumption. Consuming at the same level as one's friends should not carry derogatory meaning. How else should one relate to the Joneses if not by keeping up with them? Level spending would result from an intuitive scanning of which synchronizing adjustments to new technology are going to be possible and which are not. This concern with well-matched reciprocity explains why age has strong effects on the household's buying of new technology.

After a certain age has been reached, an individual will usually have a rough idea of what his expected scale of consumption will be. Young professionals whose salaries are relatively low by comparison with what they can earn later will develop early a larger scale of consumption than the less skilled wage earners at the same income or higher, who have already reached the peak of their earning potential and know the limits to their scale of consumption. A German survey of levels of ownership [8] among different occupational groups showed that age has strong effects on the household's current technology. They broke down three income classes into stages in the life cycle and found a close relationship between age and equipment level. Young families, regardless of income bracket, had significantly higher levels of ownership, and despite their above average equipment, the young families were not satisfied with what they had. Their aspirations to acquire more equipment outstripped those of older families with the same or higher average income. This makes sense, since after marriage and especially after mid-career, a couple knows what their expected future scale of consumption is likely to be, and nothing they can install in the way of time- and space-controlling equipment will at this late stage heave them up to a larger scale of operation. The same survey showed a larger proportion of manual workers owning household durables (refrigerator, freezer, washing machine, television) than the civil servants and professionals they were being compared with, whose average income was actually higher. Car ownership was the same in both classes. By contrast, the civil servants and professionals spent proportionately more on furniture in their homes. This suggests a more intensive social use of the home for entertaining and an attempt at "furnishing level," which corresponds to drinking level in another context of reciprocity.

The popular literature on consumption is surprisingly supercilious about attempts to be equipped at the same level. Terms such as "conspicuous consumption," "band-wagoning," "the Veblen effect," [9] and an aura of disapproval over keeping up with the Joneses puts the writers on the side of the excluders, against those who are trying not to be excluded. This may explain why the slow acceptance of the telephone among the ordinary people of Britain has received so little attention. There we observe a time-saving device which those who own it rank fourth among other time-saving necessities, which for the most part they possess anyway.

We have evidence of two populations—one is short of time, spends on saving it, and spends time and money on voluntary charitable or political organizations with friends connected by telephone; the other seems to have more time and less equipment. Two distinctive patterns of periodicity constraints pull the preference orderings apart. Answering a questionnaire, telephone subscribers ranked the telephone fourth, after vacuum cleaner, washing machine, and refrigerator; nonsubscribers ranked the telephone sixth, adding television and car to the preceding list.[10] They do not have it, so of course they rank it low; if they wanted it more, they would have it. Thus speaks the traditional theorist, relying on revealed preference. But economic man often seems to be a "satisficing animal whose problem solving is based on search activity to meet certain aspirational levels, rather than a maximizing animal whose problem solving involves finding the best alternatives in terms of specified criteria." [11] Presumably it is part of rationality to fix aspirations at some feasible level. Given the periodicities that govern my day, given the likely scale of my future consumption, given my expected permanent income, I am not likely to have friends with telephones who will telephone me, so I hardly need to install one in my home. I must seek to synchronize my consumption activities with my friends who are subject to similar periodicity constraints.

PART TWO

Implications for
Social Policy

Chapter 7

SEPARATE ECONOMIC SPHERES IN ETHNOGRAPHY

Economic Spheres

Ethnography can show clearly how patterns of frequency in social activities separate high- and low-status activities in tribal society and confer high and low value upon the objects used. Above all, tribal examples give clear demonstrations of how luxuries tend to be used as weapons of exclusion. At this stage everything in the argument seems to support the economists' puritanical bias in favor of necessities and against luxuries. Some moral reinstatement of nonnecessities must await a later stage in the argument.

Anthropologists have long been intrigued by what appear to be discrete, bounded economic spheres in small islands or isolated tribes. Elizabeth Hoyt's *Primitive Trade* [1] first drew systematic attention to these spheres. She drew many illustrations from the accounts of early travelers who needed different kinds of shell currency for different classes of transactions, even in the same village. As documentation increased, these discrete economic spheres with their nonnegotiable currencies were found to be not merely separate but also ranked, so that one sphere was more prestigious than another. Subsequently, the swelling reports of new examples have made the subject of discrete, ranked spheres of exchange in primitive economics a favorite problem of anthropologists,[2] and the whirl of complications has led one to declare that this is a problem fit to baffle economic analysis.[3] Elizabeth Hoyt, who originally noted the difficulties of travelers who could only use their stock of cornelian beads for one type of transaction, explained it by recourse to hypotheses about primitive psychology. Kroeber's well-described account of the Yurok will serve to sketch an explanation based upon technology and frequency of consumption events. Among the Yurok, separate bands of incompatible periodicities in the allocation of responsibility correspond to graded ranks. This tribe of Algonkin fishers and hunters numbered about 2,500 in the 1920s. They lived in village clusters along the lower Klamath River and along the Pacific shore in northern California. They had a culture as commercial in outlook as any modern industrial society today. Kroeber said of them:

Money is prized and establishes influence everywhere in California. It certainly counts for more in private and public life among the average Californian people than among the tribes of the plains. . . . But whatever its influence in southern or middle California, that influence is multiplied among the Yurok. Blood money, bride-purchase, compensation to the year's mourners before a dance can be held, are institutions known to almost every group described in the present work. The north-westerners alone have measured the precise value of everyman's life or wife or grief. Every injury, each privilege or wrong or trespass, is calculated and compensated. Without exactly adjusted payment, cessation of a feud is impossible except through utter extirpation of one party, marriage is not marriage but a public disgrace for generations, [and] the ceremony necessary for the preservation of the order of the world is not held. The consequence is that the Yurok concerns his life above all else with property. When he has leisure, he thinks of money; if in need, he calls upon it. He schemes constantly for opportunity to lodge a claim or to evade an obligation. No resource is too mean or too devious for him to essay in this pursuit.

If such endeavours are to be realized, there are needed an accurately computable scheme of economic valuation and an elaborate and precise code of rights. The north-western has both. A few simple and basic principles are projected into the most intricate subtleties; and there is no contingency which they do not cover.[4]

Property and rights pertain to the realm of the individual, and the Yurok recognizes no public claim and the existence of no community. His world is wholly an aggregation of individuals. There being no society as such, there is no social organization. Government being wanting, there is no authority, and without authority there can be no chief. The men so-called are individuals whose wealth, and their ability to retain and employ it, have gathered around them a collection of kinsmen, followers, and semidependents to whom they dispense assistance and protection. The power of life and death is in the hands of the rich men; for the poor man the only chance of collecting debts owed to him is to have the backing of a rich man, and the latter backs him but at the price of allegiance. The blood money to be paid on killing a rich man was 50 percent higher than that for a poor man. The charge for marrying a rich man's daughter and the damages for adultery with a rich man's wife were always higher than for poor families.

As to art and culture, Kroeber says, there was practically none here, compared with the other tribes around (who took money a little less seriously). Of masks, altars, and sacred apparatus, there were none. "The tangible paraphernalia of public ceremony are objects that possess a high property value —wealth that impresses, but nevertheless profane and negotiable wealth. The dances are displays of this wealth as much as they are song and step."[5]

There can be no question of the ethnographer being mistaken about his tribe. Kroeber knew the Californian Indian cultures like the back of his hand. His description of just where the Yurok are like and unlike their neighbors to the north and south is brief and authoritative.

In such a small society, with the five largest towns together containing just over 600 persons, and most groups of villages being able to muster only 200, we have unfettered individualism and enormous discriminations of wealth. The example would be well chosen to counter an objection that, unlike ourselves, primitive peoples always live corporate lives, submitting individual desires to the needs of the community. Their household consumption was streamed in two directions. One was the ordinary household demand for the usual services, food, fishing tackle, hunting gear, medical services, and housing. Fishing sites might also be included here. All these things had a known price in shell money, but apart from medical treatment and fishing sites, they rarely were bought for cash, but instead were obtained on claims of kinship and neighborhood. They might be counted as those consumption goods in frequent use that everyone regarded as necessary. Since the other stream involved high risks, almost gambling, it was just as well that subsistence was separated and treated as an independent sphere. The second stream consisted of treasures valued in and substitutable for shell money: obsidian blades, rare pelts and colored feathers for dancing paraphernalia on public occasions, and boats. The shell money, in lengths of about 27 inches, were avidly sought after and passionately accumulated. With shell money each man contested with every other man his right to a place in society, to avenge insults, to marry his daughters to respected citizens, and to have his own little following of dependents. This was the political sphere,[6] attracting all the most important marking services. At prodigious dance displays, the rich man would decorate himself in these white deerskins and woodpecker scalps and show off his obsidian blades. No man could enter the political arena if his subsistence was not assumed. But subsistence alone would be unthinkable for a man without this second stream of wealth for transacting politically with other men. So for every Yurok man his welfare could be separated into two distinct parts, one domestic and one political, each with its distinctive periodicities and its relevant group of goods. Within the group of domestic goods there was substitutability, and complementarity; likewise within the group of political goods, but the two groups could be treated as practically independent. A good run of salmon or a bad year for berries made no difference to the demand for shells and for goods within the set relevant to the exchange of shells.

TABLE 7-1
Yurok Household Consumption

egular Feasts, nes, and Fees	Sphere of Political Goods Substitutable for Each Other at Standard Exchange Rates	Shells Obsidian Blades Deer Pelts Woodpecker Feathers Boats	Low-Frequency, High Rank Activities Involving Large Units
ily Needs	Sphere of Domestic Goods and Services Freely Exchangeable for Each Other	House Fishing Sites and Game Areas Gear Fishing Hunting Food Fish Game Vegetable Products	High-Frequency, Low Rank Activities Involving Small Units

This diagram shows a jump in value for the Yurok as between the two sets of goods. The domestic goods in high-frequency use posed no problem of distribution. No one went short of food unless there was a general shortage. A man in heavy debt might be forced to sell a fishing site, but this would be because of insolvency only less grave than the case in which he might have to sell himself—both unusual situations resulting from a general lack of support and credit-worthiness. Demand pressed heavily on the low-frequency political goods, the means of giving and getting valued marking services. At the top of the society were the leaders, the richest men. No one in his right mind would give up political treasure for domestic goods since the rate of return on loaning the former or otherwise laying it out was immensely greater than what could be expected from domestic goods. Collaboration among close kinsmen reigned in domestic goods, and competition among rivals in political goods, as Cora Dubois explains for a parallel case. Thus the discrete economic spheres here described pose no mystery. They can easily be interpreted by economic analysis. But the special interest of this case is the clear illustration of the principles set out in the last chapter. Based upon periodicities in consumption use, exactly as we would expect, there appears a strong separation between two classes of goods, such that rates of substitution between any pairs in one group are insulated from changes in quantities of any goods in the other group.

Scale of Consumption

The example can be used to make an advance in the argument. Whereas a connection has been indicated between high status of goods and low frequency of use and vice versa, and whereas there were obviously difficulties in making an analysis of all the relevant patterns of periodicity, the Yurok example suggests that the concept of scale of consumption activities would be a convenient shorthand for compressing these several related characteristics. Low-frequency, high-ranking activities involving large social units and necessarily putting those engaged in them into contact with the centers of power and influence can well be called a large-scale consumption pattern and can be assumed to be very advantageous for getting and controlling information. High-frequency, low-ranking activities involving small social units constitute a small-scale consumption pattern, disadvantageous for getting and controlling information. We have argued that assumptions of rationality lead us to expect the individual to aim at the large-scale type of consumption pattern, and the Yurok exemplify such striving. Theoretically they were an egalitarian society. They had no chiefs, no aristocrats. Anyone could enter the lists and everyone did. This does not mean that wealth was distributed evenly. An accelerator principle ensured that any initial advantage would lead to an increased scale of operations, and thus worked cumulatively to the further advantage of the lucky beneficiary. Thomas Mayer illustrates the point from the case of two pianists. Whatever the distribution of native ability, he says, the distribution of earnings will be more positively skewed than the distribution of abilities because the latter are reinforced by differences in the scale of operation. The abler of two pianists will have a higher income for two multiplicative reasons, first because people are willing to pay more for a ticket, and second because he will play in a larger hall.[7] Likewise among the Yurok the rich man got richer and the poor man poorer because the rich man had more followers, and more followers entitled him to demand higher rates of pay for his services, making him richer and therefore able to attract more followers. The Yurok rich man did not need to set up barriers restricting admission to the ranks of privilege. Everyone could compete, and the rules of the competition itself, like the market principle, secured further comparative advantages for those who started out well endowed.

Refusal to Transact

Other examples of discrete spheres of exchange in tribal society show how they can be formed as monopolistic barriers controlling admission.

The Tiv of the lower Benue river, Nigeria, are alleged to have had three such separate spheres before European money wrecked their system.[8] The top-ranking one contained only rights over women. Access to it was so closely restricted that any suspicion of trying to buy a wife with material wealth would be scandalous. The Tiv "elders," influential men, not so very old but heads of lineages, transacted with one another, using rights over women for forging a network of alliances and making sure that anyone admitted as a son-in-law showed the right disposition and entrepreneurial talent. The next high-ranking sphere included metal rods, bales of cloth, guns, and slaves, all to be obtained by war or trade. Active young men acquired these goods and presumably paid them into the equivalent of the lineage treasury, getting thereby a good reputation among their seniors and the backing needful for marriage alliance. Or they may have used them to exert direct influence in the market and become "elders" themselves.[9] The lowest-ranking sphere was again the domestic one. There, chickens, hoes, baskets, pots, and grain could be exchanged for one another.

In this case again, though women worked in the domestic sphere, their men were responsible for them and used rights over them for advancing their interests. Men alone worked the prestige sphere. The domestic sphere was high frequency, low status in its normal activities, and the other was low frequency, high status. And as in the case of the Yurok, by energy and vigilance in the prestige sphere, a man acquired wives as well as politically useful alliances. So the problem allegedly posed by a barrier of nonconvertibility between the spheres, which has so much exercised anthropologists, disappears. The only

TABLE 7-2
Tiv Household Transactions

a.	Marriage Alliance — Rights Over Women	
b.	Prestige Goods	
	Metal	
	Cloth	Low-Frequency Transactions
	Guns	Involving Large Social Units,
	Slaves	High Rank
	Cattle	
c.	Domestic Goods	
	Baskets	
	Pots	High-Frequency Transactions
	Hoes	Involving Small Units,
	Grain	Low Rank
	Chickens	

economic sense it would make for a Tiv man to agree to exchange precious guns or slaves for umpteen hundred baskets of chickens or grain would be if he planned on going into the chicken or grain business, but there was no profit to be gained that way. In such an imperfect market it was clearly more profitable to invest directly in prestige goods rather than in low-ranking chickens or grain. Keeping their sights on marriageable girls was better economic sense, as Trollope would have been the first to agree. Ultimately, the two big discontinuities arise from monopolistic barriers to entry. The elders had everything to gain by keeping tight control of the marriageable women, and they rightly refused to be tempted out of their corner by material considerations. Their political advantages meant that they were in control of the information system and had every incentive to stay there. Two things kept their privileges secure: one, their refusal to transact rights over women with outsiders; the other, their use of control over women for drawing the wealth in the second economic sphere into their control as representatives of the lineage. This is our own interpretation of the Tiv material, as Bohannan does not link this analysis of economic and political behavior (land rights, market control, and warfare) so closely to lineage control of women, which had been considerably disrupted by the time of his fieldwork. This synthesis is suggested by parallel researches among the Lele.[10]

One way to maintain a social boundary is to demand an enormous fee for admission. Another is to set the normal rate for settling of internal transactions so high that only the very rich can afford to join the game. The Yurok system was something like that, since a man needed great wealth in shells and rare valuables to enter the dance societies. A third way is simply to decline to transact with outsiders. Refusal to transact is such a common, if not worldwide, strategy of exclusion that we have been able to base a cross-cultural meaning for the notion of consumption. Consumption has been here defined as that area of social relations in which transactions are made freely, by the free election of the partners, constrained by nothing but their perception of their own intentions, beyond the law and beyond commerce. The Tiv put the transfer of women in marriage beyond commerce. They affected to despise neighboring tribes who accepted marriage payments for their daughters. In truth these other tribes also put marriage beyond commerce and did not reckon that by accepting the equivalent of a dowry from their son-in-law's family they were in any way selling brides. Their marriage transactions were no doubt just as restricted and they kept as firm a hold on admission to the status of relative in-law. But by their total refusal to transact women for goods, the Tiv could keep the whole intricate lineage structure in gerontocratic hands, and it may be that in the precolonial period only the disturbance of major wars gave the up-and-coming young warrior a chance to jump ahead of his generation into the ranks of elderhood and control. Bohannan suggests that the advent of European money, with its power to permeate all transactions, brought the collapse of the social system. But in the case of the Lele, the old men effectively resisted the infiltrations of money. If they had not refused to accept Belgian francs for marriage payments, always insisting on settlement in kind, they would have lost control of the marriageable girls, for the young men could earn francs and they could not. Their intransigence even produced a double exchange rate against the franc and a 10 percent discount for settlement in kind for all debts.[11]

Restricted Circulation

Now there appears nothing inexplicable, mysterious, or contrary to traditional economic theory about restricted economic spheres. The energy to protect boundaries from unwanted arbitrage is stoked by the sense of how much is at risk—personal survival in a competitive scene or collective survival in a whole system of values and traditions. Restricted circulation is not likely to flourish except as an element of the total system of work and reward.

At first sight the craze of the rich women traders of the Hausa Quarter of Ibadan for highly colored imported pots seems an irrational desire, a quirk of consumer tastes. And so it was, in respect of the colored pots themselves; the women's fancy could have lit on anything else: the choice of a material thing for a form of currency can well be fairly arbitrary. Their insatiable buying of more and more pots is fully explicable if the collection of pots, divisible, standardized, durable, storable, and portable, is interpreted as the currency for a restricted sphere of exchange.

In a chapter entitled "Trade from Behind the Purdah," Abner Cohen explains that the Moslem Hausa of Ibadan normally kept their womenfolk secluded.[12] One who wished for a private career as a prostitute had freedom to walk where she liked, but paradoxically this did not give her the opportunity to amass wealth that the respectable matrons enjoyed. The Hausa Quarter was in the 1960s a flourishing trade center, thronging with bachelors and strangers, all needing to be fed. The married woman could enter a profitable catering industry, cooking and selling food. For this she needed labor and capital. Her own daughters and the daughters of kinsfolk and even the children of foreigners fostered by her would run her errands and do her work and she would be expected eventually to help them to make suitable marriages. For capital she had three sources, an initial gift made at marriage, savings from the household money allotted by her husband, and the profits of trade. She would run a business with practically no overhead expenses, since her husband paid the rent and fed and clothed her. If she could develop a steady clientele, she could amass a great deal of wealth. But the social structure that ordained her seclusion ordained at the same time that there would be no way of investing her wealth in other forms of business, for catering was the only thing that did not compete with men. So it was understandable that a special consumption pattern should develop, shared only by married women traders, and, further, that this should become the public testing of each other's business success and credit-worthiness. Women could own houses and could hoard cash and jewelry,

But the particular craze among nearly all the housewives in recent years has been to sink all their profits in acquiring ever increasing numbers of Czechoslovak-made brightly coloured enamel bowls. Within the world of Sabo housewives, these bowls have become the most important status symbol and women are ranked in status according to the number of bowls they possess. Some housewives in the Quarter have managed to accumulate hundreds of them, which they meticulously arrange in ceiling-high columns in their small, dark rooms. A business landlord invited my wife to visit his two wives, but these asked him to fix the time of the proposed visit at a date which would give them nearly two weeks' grace during which they could wash and rearrange their treasured bowls. Space is scarce in Sabo, and husbands are greatly annoyed by the mountains of bowls. A current sardonic complaint among married men of the Quarter is that, because of the bowls, a man cannot nowadays find space in his wife's room for even his morning prayers.

A housewife thus accumulates bowls and when her own daughters or her foster-daughters get married she gives them part of her treasure, usually in proportion to the length of time the daughter has served her.[13]

It all sounds crazy, irrational, puppet consumption if ever there was any. But the ethnographer does not fall into the trap of treating utility as quite independent of earning ability. "A housewife will attract and retain more marriageable girls from her kin the more bowls she accumulates. The older a woman is, the more settled as a housewife she becomes and the more girls she attracts to her service." The connection between consumption and production is crystal clear.

Control over the Economy

In these cases and in many more that can be cited, the refusal to transact or the refusal to accept payment except in particular currencies does more than protect a privilege. The boundary being protected in effect encircles the whole structure of the economy, production, and consumption. Control of the whole social system, no less, may be at stake. When this point is fully appreciated, the theory of consumption can be detrivialized and reintegrated into the analysis of the whole economy.

Individual luxuries, acquired by themselves, signal nothing in particular. But a consistent array, understood by the other consumers, at least signals credit-worthiness. If it is not one interlocking series of objects, it will be another.

Among the rich pot-collecting women traders of Sabo, credit-worthiness was easily traced to its financial nexus in their system of production. But in the theory of consumption that best suits anthropological materials, the track is usually more roundabout. It is characterized by a more diffuse respectability, a sense of occasion, the signs of ability to discriminate finely and to know the social scene from top to bottom that brings in marking services and identifies the superconsumer who cannot be left out of any major celebration. This kind of social creditworthiness is perfectly well known and needs no underlining. But a few implications are more hidden. The Sabo ladies were frankly commercial in their dominant interests: enforced seclusion from the rest of society narrowed their scope, and correspondingly their choice of luxuries was confined. For freer individuals the main characteristic of a luxury is that it forms part of a widely varied range of goods. The one-luxury man is a poor man. As a man gets richer his most income-responsive buying habits diversify, and one should consider the total structure of his luxuries if one is to understand their nature. One of the many advantages of being relatively rich is that when a drop in income enforces economy, there is a whole series of goods which are only weakly interdependent on each other and which each can be considered for cuts. Economists normally assume that this diversity arises because the possibility of getting enjoyment out of increasing units of any one good declines with the quantity available of that good. But I will argue that it has an information aspect. The ladies of Sabo were insatiable where their collection of pots was concerned. They could not have too many. If they had a richer social life, plausibly they would have wanted other things as well as pots to show their visitors and to give as wedding presents.

There are two points to be made concerning luxuries as consumption goods in an information system. One is that in a highly diverse society, the demand for luxuries has to be correspondingly diversified: each item sends its signal, but each also represents a special field of social relations with its appropriate consumption activity. As far as information goes the rich individual has more finely attuned reception and signaling by the goods he can use. Their very diversity is an important fact about luxuries, each the latest word in style and comfort in a highly specialized activity. The second is, paradoxically, their tendency to be standardized, as any public person going out to dinner on public ceremonial events will testify: the same hors d'oeuvres, the same pheasant and salmon according to season, the same vegetables and desserts followed by the same small sips of concentrated hot and cold liquids. It is as if the current formula for high-ranking occasions cannot be tampered with at risk of giving wrong signals.[14]

What is the point about this tendency to standardize? It seems likely that it would not arise except where close comparisons of value are required. At the fringes of a market system, where turnover is slower, where knowledge is incomplete, and big profits riskier, discrepancies in standards can pass. But where the competition is hottest, standardization emerges. The Sabo women have standardized on Czechoslovakian enamel pots, a field they can master completely. In the Trobriands, exchange of Kula objects is closely standardized: only two kinds of item are acceptable, red shell beads and white shell armbands. The items are known individually and their relative value can be established since everyone in the circle is a connoisseur.[15] Among the Yurok, as we saw, only certain classes of goods count as equivalents, and their rate of substitution is precisely known. When the tendency to standardize values is strong, some crucial form of social control is being exerted: it is a sign that we are near the hot center of a competitive system where small differences matter a lot.

The ethnography of distant tribes may lull the reader into complacency. But that would be a pity. If production and consumption are shown as part of a circular process, the accusing finger that points at production must point just as truly at consumption behavior. A myriad of self-interested refusals to transact (whether by not joining wedding feasts or beer-drinking) could undo the effects of redistributive legislation as it affects wealth holding and consequent advancement. For consumption, insofar as it depends on the principle of strictly judged reciprocity, is like a market from whose ranks the less efficient members can be driven down successively to less exacting and less rewarding echelons.

Chapter 8

INTERNATIONAL COMPARISONS

Separable Demand for Goods

Clear though the lesson of the last chapter may be, its application to ourselves may yet be obscure. The tribes that are cited are distant, small, and exotic. We are all the other things, near, large, and so familiar that it is hard to see that the separate economic spheres which emerge, in their case, to give strongly partitioned groupings of goods can ever work like that here.

Let us summarize the advances that have been made. From seeing how the technology of consumption responds to the demand for personal availability, and from noting the correlation between ranking and certain frequencies in consumption patterns, we get a concept of scale of consumption. Large scale, high rank, this means having access to and control of the information necessary to maintain income. The information approach we are developing implies that the consumer will be rational to aim at large-scale consumption. The ethnographic cases show a tendency for successful entrants to put up protective barriers around the circle in which they control information. Partitioning among goods appears clearly as the expression of social partitioning and results in big discrepancies in the scale of consumption.

It would seem to follow that to search for partitions among goods without scrutinizing the structure of society is a waste of time. A final lesson from the ethnographic cases is that the top rank in a stratified system is often a very rarefied sphere, austere from the point of view of material objects. Among the Tiv at the top rank, when rights for women were exchanged, goods were expressly excluded. Among the Hausa women, consumption does not wear out the valued goods; the exchange of marking services consists in inviting friends to come and have a look. Among the Trobrianders, where precious Kula objects circulate between high-ranking men, the most precious are the oldest, which have been transferred the most carefully and hardly ever displayed. Their names are known, and it is an honor to have one's own name associated with the name of a famous valuable. Indeed, what is being transacted in the top sphere is really shared knowledge about a network of mutual confidence. The actual goods are the visible tip of the iceberg. The rest is a submerged classified catalogue of names of persons, places, objects, and dates. The main activity is a continuous attempt to standardize their values as precisely as possible.

What is being held in the top sphere, and contained there as far as possible, is creativity. Alternative ways of doing things may be glimpsed, alternative kinds of knowledge may be hinted, but here in the privileged circle of top-rank superconsumers, decisions are made about sponsoring. To sponsor is to support the channeling of resources. Without substantial material support, the hints and glimpses of other possibilities will stay unrealized. Here, in the top-ranking sphere, where knowledge is put under control, reallocative possibilities are scanned, naturally from a strictly interested point of view.

It would be laboring a point already made to insist again that when they look for principles for grouping goods, economists are on the wrong track if they look at the physical properties of the goods. They are also likely to be on the wrong trail if they concentrate exclusively on small-scale consumption activities: there is little hope of understanding how poverty arises or what it feels like if we do not understand the rich. They are likely to be off the track if they focus only on what goes on inside the individual household and do not apply their measuring rods to map systematically the relationships of households with other households. The economists working on consumption as part of a household production process [1] think of the household as producing services for itself from combined inputs of time and of cash-bought goods. They explicitly include in the analysis marking services from other households. But the results of the exercise tend to be disappointing because the conditions for getting marking services [2] are not analyzed.

The question of the relevance of economic anthropology to our own case turns upon whether anything like distinct spheres of consumption may be found in this country in this day and age. It can be maintained that in the study of relatively short-term market behavior an adequate explanation can be formulated in terms of income distribution, prices, and household size and composition, and when these have all been properly taken into account, the explanation of consumption behavior is practically complete.[3] In terms of average national behavior, this may be true—insofar as we are a class-stratified society, the differences must be found in the production side of the economy, which determines the distribution of earnings and wealth. It further implies that if those differences were eliminated we would get sizable differences in consumption only between big and small families, between employed and unemployed, and that would be about all. However, the argument from ethnography is that we would do well to trace the powerful, spontaneous forces of exclusion which arise to control and protect any valuable resources and which would continually tend to make new divisions in society. Indeed, we can go one stage further and claim that the ethnographic parallel is more relevant to economic understanding of our own consumption behavior now than it ever was before. For in the earlier phases of the history of economic thought, land was first held to be the source of wealth and power, and then labor, with both assumptions directing attention to production. But now that attention is focused upon technical know-how, the place of education becomes equivocal.[4] Education is not consumption but has to be counted as investment in human capital. Technological advance is reckoned the essential factor that gives comparative advantage in international trade.[5] By a quirky paradox we are back full-swing to the economic state of primitive societies where inside knowledge in a swiftly changing scene is the main factor in getting the lead in competition for control. And the previous chapter shows that consumption is far from neutral in this contest.

That which disguises itself as a disinterested, friendly, hospitable consumption sphere in practice draws up dividing lines between those in control and those they are excluding. The ethnography suggests that we will find these consumption spheres, distinct and ranked, here as well as among the Tiv and the Yurok, and that these should yield a basis for discerning groupings among goods.

This scheme needs some explanation if it is to serve as a bridge between the ethnography of the last chapter and our own case. Consumption scale in the first column is described in the second and third columns. Among the Tiv, the difference between small and large scale applies most obviously to the difference between men and women; the fact that women alone are subject to periodicity constraints in itself frees the men for warfare, trade, and politics. The reference to large units in the third column means either that the ritual is on a massive scale, or that, if it is select, each consumer represents some large

TABLE 8-1
Consumption Spheres

Consumption Scale	Periodicity Constraints in Household Processes	Frequency of Major Consumption Rituals Involving Large Units
Small	Heavy Constraints, High-Frequency Household Routines	Infrequent
Medium	Less Periodicity Constraints, Improved Technology Basis of Consumption	Infrequent and Excluded from Circulation of Marking Services in Larger-Scale Consumption Circles
Large	Freedom from Periodicity Constraints Thanks to Improved Technology or Employment of Domestic Labor	Frequent, Involving Large Units and Monopolistically Excluding Middle and Low Ranks

social interest, his lineage, and political faction, or in the case of the Sabo women traders, a large personal network potentially supplying child labor to the hostess. The information that is exchanged on such occasions by means of display is consequently weightier and relates to the economic and political *status quo*.

If there are such social spheres in the modern industrial society, there is no need to prejudge the question of whether the top sphere is deliberately and consciously excluding with a view to exercising monopoly. The pattern of life based on different periodicities in itself makes a natural if unintended barrier to free social intercourse. And then there is the pernicious reciprocity rule. The same principle which makes "an eye for an eye and a tooth for a tooth" the harshest rule in the Old Testament makes a harsh principle of separation in consumption. Where reciprocity applies (and it seems to be pretty universally accepted as the principle for fair dealing), like goods are exchanged within each sphere. So reciprocity in itself is a principle of exclusion. When the Sabo women go to admire each other's enamel pots, the ethnographer is amazed that the pots are all so similar. In the same spirit Malinowski noted that the Kula objects prized by the Trobriand Islanders were closely standardized, with the hint of surprise that the exchange did not achieve the usual objectives of trade. He followed a native distinction in treating the Kula exchange as something very different from the various forms of barter which the islanders practiced. In barter, inland villages exchanged their yams for fish provided by the shore dwellers and islands exchanged the products of their specialized skills or regional resources. The exchange rested upon difference, whereas where the Kula objects were concerned, it took a connoisseur's eye to spot the differences. And with ourselves it takes a trained eye to recognize the difference between one wedding cake or silver teapot and another.

Here again a change in economic theory makes the ethnographic case more like ourselves than before. Linder's model of international trade would divide it up into two kinds.[6] That which takes place among the developed and technologically advanced countries rests upon the similarity of demand structure in each of the trading countries. They exchange the same kind of goods, highly standardized, with minute variations. He gives sound reasons for understanding the disadvantages in such a trade and the difficulties of breaking into it experienced by a country with a very different demand pattern. The argument is very close (but much more fully worked out) to that by which we could explain the emergence of different spheres of consumption, based on differences in periodicities and technology. The second kind of foreign trade described by Linder conforms to the traditional theory in that the basis of exchange is difference. This usually means an undeveloped country exporting primary products to a developed country. All the inequalities and disadvantages resulting from assymmetrical exchange in anthropological records [7] are found and analyzed in this type of foreign trade.

Poor Individuals and Poor Countries

In several ways the example of international trade seems useful to the understanding of consumption. Its old theoretical apparatus has come to the same pass as utility theory in being judged both powerful and useless. Economists themselves see its gears grinding away without meshing with reality. At the same time a very empirical spirit of investigation is developing new ways of thinking about exchange and its effects. What it is like to be a poor household is probably very parallel to the plight of a poor nation.

We can start by following the usual classification of economic activities. This defines three major sectors of employment:

primary: agriculture, hunting, forestry, and fishing
secondary: mining and quarrying, manufacturing, electricity, gas, water, and construction
tertiary: commerce, transport, storage and communication, financing, insurances, real estate and business services, community, social, and personal services (other activities not adequately defined) [8]

The primary sector depends on natural resources, the other two on varying combinations of capital and skills. Most of the secondary sector depends on intensive use of both skill and capital. The tertiary sector depends mostly on special skills. It will be of special interest to our comparison of spheres of consumption, for the development of a big tertiary sector also draws together the policy-making and manipulative capacity for the economic system as a whole.

The changes involved in economic development gradually

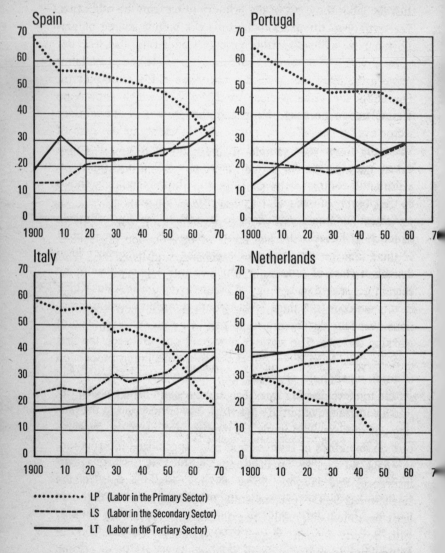

FIGURE 8-1
Decline of the Primary Sector

From the *International Standard Industrial Classification of Economic Activities.* New York: Statistical Office of the United Nations; cited in *The Service Industries,* by Yves Sabalo, pp. 12, 21, and 22. Geneva: ILO, 1975.

shift the labor force out of the primary sector into the other two. The tertiary sector tends to become the largest source of employment in a developed economy. Comparing the less developed with the developed countries, the distribution of labor between the three sectors in a country shows the same pattern. The shifts are visually clear in figure 8–1 which shows the decline in the primary sector and the growth of the tertiary sector over a period of economic development. In the case of Spain the three lines crossed only in the 1960s; in Portugal in the same period the primary sector is still the largest; and a dramatic contrast between Italy and the Netherlands shows up the poverty of one and the prosperity of the other.[9]

Almost the same pattern is to be drawn for the economic structure of households. The poor households must spend most of their time getting food and preparing it. At the next level there is a class of household which is well equipped with the current household technology of labor-saving devices, but which is very weak at the third level, where interhousehold transactions over long distances keep in play a continuous exchange of marking services. The analogy is a good one. Between the first and the third level there will show up the declining proportion of total expenditure allocated to food, supporting Engel's law. At the top level the family of Engel curves will have splayed out into a wide range of tertiary activities that correspond to the putting out of household work to laundries and cleaners, expenditure on any kinds of services that relay specialized information, journals, education, financial advice, brokers, estate agents, insurance, and lawyers. Some of the questions that remain unanswered in the present state of poverty studies could at least be stated differently by continuing to press the analogy with poverty among nations. For example, the problem of getting people out of poverty is not how to get them enough to eat and drink; this is the condition for sustaining people in poverty. Usually the primary sector is all too well represented; the problem is how to expand the secondary and tertiary sectors, especially the latter.

The Gap

Economists are not agreed as to whether the gap between rich and poor in this country is increasing, decreasing, or stable. As far as real income is concerned, there is no doubt that everyone is better off. By 1938 the real income of the average working class family was 37 percent higher than it had been in 1913.[10] As to earnings, there has recently been a slight reduction in the ratio of highest to lowest earnings.[11] But "income poverty" persists. Low-paid work is the lot of a persistently large proportion of the total labor force. Any earnings distribution will have a bottom tenth. But how big is the gap between their earnings and the rest? For the United Kingdom between 1886 and 1971, the National Board of Prices and Incomes [12] reported that the dispersion of earnings had hardly changed—in a period in which money earnings had increased twentyfold. The bottom decile of earnings of full-time manual workers was never less than 66.5 percent of the median. Other facts suggest a bottom layer of manual workers whose relative social position stays the same as the level of their pay in relation to the rest of the country.[13] In the United States it is questionable whether the extent of intergenerational status mobility has changed over the last half century. International comparisons indicate that the problem is the same among the relatively rich countries, capitalist and socialist alike: the extent of intergenerational immobility is much the same everywhere, and feeds on processes that are common to advanced countries in the modern era.[14] Certainly poverty leads to a declining spiral of well-being in which the costs of improvement go up with every twist. "Poverty is not a discrete condition: the constriction of choice becomes progressively more damaging in a continuous manner." [15] Those with the lowest incomes live in the poorest neighborhoods, they cannot afford economies of scale, their shopping is high frequency, and for the tiny quantities they buy they pay higher retail prices. Their borrowing costs them marginally more, pound for pound.[16] Welfare programs proposed for their benefit tend to do more for the children of middle-class homes for whom they provide employment.[17] The structure of earnings in other industrial countries shows a stable pattern similar to the United Kingdom's. Redistributive legislation, education, and other efforts seem to have little success in disturbing it; attention turns naturally from incomes to the pattern of wealth holding. "The difference between the top wealth holders and the average person (let alone those whose wealth is below the average) is much greater than in the case of earnings. The magnitude of gap is in fact quite staggering."[18] Wealth gives great advantages and it gives a measure of control over the structure of society. Consequently, a comparison of the distribution of wealth between Britain and other industrial countries seems to promise a more direct way of understanding poverty than a comparison of the dispersal of earnings. But the statistics for comparing wealth are sadly ambiguous, and methods of collecting these statistics vary from country to country. There are different principles for calculating the comparisons. Underlying these sources of controversy is a weakness in the basic materials of the calculations. People are partly reluctant to disclose their savings; mostly they just do not know their own net worth. It tends to be revealed, often as a surprise, only at death. So while it is a move in the right direction to seek to compare wealth rather than annual income, and while it would be much more revealing of social trends if the comparison could be standardized and made accurate, the data is so difficult to measure as to be full of traps for the unwary anthropologist.

Less Developed Consumption

If we could blow the individual household up to the size of a nation, we might see what the same problem looks like in gross. At least in international trade a consensus appears among the economists as to the gap between rich and poor nations: without mystery or doubt, this gap has widened phenomenally and seems likely to go on widening (with the recent difference that the oil-producing countries have shifted from one side of the line to the other).

At first glance, private income for the household looks like the correct equivalent to per capita product for a nation. But second thoughts show up an illusion here. What flows into the household as income only sets part of the floor and a ceiling to consumption possibilities. The rest of the product depends on varied combinations of time and money, and the cherishing of work or family or other social values. It would be a mistake to treat private income as the household equivalent of a nation's per capita product. Money income is only the cash input to the household; if anything, it is more like the wages bill for the nation. We cannot hope to devise a digit that will compare total household consumption accurately with national per capita product. Marking services, by their very nature, as we saw in defining them, resist such accountability. We shall have to invent some crude device so as to make further comparison fruitful. But as it happens, per capita product is not the most central concept in international comparisons; it is an index of structural differences. In comparing the gap between rich and poor nations, it is not the total per capita product in money terms, nor the heterogeneous pile of their real products, but their scale of operations that is the basic structural difference. So our use of the concept of scale of consumption will probably be as good a crude device as any for continuing the comparison.

The parallel between individuals and nations still has to be pursued with caution. Yet we have shown that there is a similarity in technological structure for nations and individual households, a striking parallel in respect of periodicities and other aspects of economic organization. These can be drawn out very instructively if the whole economic performance of the nation is carefully compared with the consumption patterns of the individual household. A traditional enough method for the comparison can be developed. It would disregard the way the individual spends working time; once the income reaches the household, its management of its affairs is then to be compared to relevant economic processes of the nation. The gap between rich and poor nations can be measured in terms of per capita product, but the meaning of the difference is much better understood as structural, technological, and cognitive. With increasing real income, the parallels between household and nation emerge; the secular tendency for the household to be putting out more and more of its traditional work to the external market is parallel to the tendency for a developing country to be reducing its subsistence sector. The richest countries have the most diversified trade outlets, the most diversified patterns of production, the biggest services sector (which includes financial, research, teaching, and administrative services). The poorest countries are most likely to be spending their energies on one product, probably low-yield agriculture. The possibility of having manpower available for other activities is as limited as the personal availability for other people's consumption rituals of members of a household committed to high-frequency processes. "Product per worker in the agricultural sector is so distressingly low as to tie to the land at low income levels a large part of the population and leave little margin for the non-agricultural sector to grow upon." [19] The rich nations are essentially those whose economy and society are geared to utilizing the technology potential of modern economic growth. If rich is taken to be equivalent to developed, and poor to undeveloped, then the gap between rich and poor is not fully understood if attention focuses on total command over goods and services. The essential distinction is between two kinds of economic structure: on the one hand, industrialized, urbanized, and mechanized economies, with the distinctive institutions that support industrial growth; and on the other hand, the others, not industrialized, not mechanized, and not tending toward growth.

Simon Kuznets has demonstrated this point very carefully,

showing that important structural differences themselves determine the value of per capita product. Characterizing the developed countries by an index that combines level of output with degree of industrialization (and including Japan among them), he calculated that 26 percent of world population in 1965 was producing 79 percent of world product, and the less developed countries (53 percent of world population)' were producing 7.9 percent of world product. He shows that over the last hundred years the countries which he counts as developed have quintupled their per capita product, while the less developed countries' per capita product rose by two-thirds at best. In one hundred years the gap has tripled in size. In that time the less developed countries were not stationary, but even if they had quadrupled their per capita product, the absolute and relative gap would still have widened.[20]

Since the gap between rich and poor countries can be so effectively described in terms of economic structure, and since these are essentially the same as the terms we use to compare consumption patterns of individual households, and since the gap in international comparisons is indisputably widening, it must be rewarding to ask what processes are discerned that might also be found in the operation of households.

Running ahead of the argument, and leaping some fences, it seems that rich households form an exchange sphere in which close similarity in life-styles permits easy reciprocity and in which reciprocal exchanges flow right through their circle without impediment, so that each is well linked with the others. To be rich means to be well integrated in a rich community. We leave aside the case of the council-house pensioner or person on relief who dies leaving thousands of pounds stashed away in the bank: he may be a poor man who has acquired money, a different case altogether. Being rich means that credit is forthcoming, that minor losses can be absorbed; it implies a web of mutual involvement which is hard to tear. To be poor is to be isolated.

Though it may seem to, this does not conflict with the popular idea of warmly intimate social life in the working class street enshrined for sociologists in the Bethnal Green studies.[21] Nor does this conflict with the equally important idea that middle class life, though well endowed materially, is relatively impoverished in respect of local community ties.[22] Both ideas are mainly concerned with family relationships, and these are not the main issue here. Not even the cozy familiarity of the street is relevant, except that Bethnal Green regards the next district as foreign parts. At issue here is the social connection between the street community and the rest of the district, the district with the rest of the city. (Of course, the man who does not even belong to the street is a very poor man indeed.)

The concept of social integration needs to be further elaborated. The tertiary sector of a rich country can act as the institutional support system of financial and administrative channels, increasing the effective scale of every activity that is built upon it. It can provide the social overhead capital that services the rest: elements within the developed economy are connected through the tertiary sector, but particular industries in the other sectors are also more closely connected with one another than they are in less developed countries. Returning to the level of the individual household, it would seem that the economic structure of the poor household not only lacks an equivalent of the tertiary sector, but it is also weak in the equivalent of the secondary sector, and its expenditure hardly links it into the largest social system at all.

Linkage

As we have been describing it, the consumer's objective is to operate a coherent information system by using marking services. His need for goods serves his more direct need to be included meaningfully with fellow consumers. The basic problem in poverty turns on the kind of mutual involvement that holds between individuals. This is why it is misleading to use a "quantity of goods" criterion of poverty. The Sudanese tribesmen with only their herds of cattle do not regard themselves as poverty-stricken. If poverty derives from failure in forms of relatedness, it may be useful to look again at studies of international trade, where measures of relatedness have been elaborated.

In the industrial structure, a key sector is defined by the degree of interrelatedness with the rest. In a key sector an innovation would have more repercussions than it would in a sector with a lesser degree of interrelatedness.[23] This can be made parallel with the idea of an individual with a strong personal network who can get attention for his opinions, hear what is going on, and so get the most out of the deployment of his goods on marking services.

Sectors of industry are linked with others in various ways. The term "backward linkage" refers to the dependence of a given industry on other industries. It is a measure of the direct use of the factors of production in a country. For example, in Malaysia exports of primary products (rubber, tin, palm oil) have given rise to a light engineering industry. In the course of time the building of tin dredges, oil palm mills, and so on, has been developed locally. Foreign firms have provided design facilities, but local producers have held their own in manufacturing. So the export of primary products became supported by backward linkage into light engineering which developed as an industry in its own right.[24] Backward linkage is assessed by computing the ratio of purchased units to the value of the total demand for a given product. "Forward linkage" means the dependence of other industries on a given industry. It is assessed by computing the ratio of intermediate to total demand for a product. Foreign trade, if it operates only in a very segregated sector of a developing country, may be harmful instead of prospering it.

The concept of linkage and its theoretical implications are very complex. There is no point in trying slavishly to copy these analytical tools. But they suggest ways of working out a measure of the consumer's involvement with the rest of the economy. We can start by constructing three kinds of consumer's linkage. Roughly corresponding with backward linkage would be what we may call consumer's technological linkage—access to and use of current technological resources. Research would aim to show up differences in the command of contemporary technology. Every few years a different set of services would need to be chosen to assess it. For example, the *Ministry of Power Statistical Digest* gives the number of electricity consumers in the United Kingdom for each year since 1948. At that time the number of households with electricity as a percentage of all households indicated the division between urban and rural population. It rose from 76.67 percent in 1948 to 97.28 percent in 1970, and so it no longer represents that division. In 1948, 23 percent of homes in the United Kingdom were unable to use the periodicity-controlling and power-increasing appliances which depended on electricity and would therefore earn a low rating for technological linkage. But after 1970 wiring should not be used as a discriminator of technological linkage because nearly every home was wired. Admittedly, strong technological linkage is only a small part of the story. A household that owned every conceivable kind of new equipment could yet be socially very isolated.

To correspond roughly with forward linkage in international trade, we would want to indicate the volume of social interaction. Consumers' social linkage could be assessed by some expenditure indicating the dependence of other homes for their consumption rituals upon the marking services produced in a given home. Relevant expenditure testifying to reciprocal sharing of consumption would be the bill for private travel, the telephone account, the amount of extra cutlery, plates, spare beds, the expenditure on entertainment, charities, clubs, church, and toys for children's friends and friends' children. A family could be heavily engaged in social linkage and poor in technological linkage—the rating would indicate different lifestyles. The analysis of international trade has also gained much from considering the advantages and disadvantages of dispersal or concentration of industries and trading partners. For the individual consumer the corresponding idea would be a sub-branch of social linkage. It would be important to know whether the marking services were all being transacted within a small geographical radius (geographical concentration), only between members of a family (social concentration), or within or across generations (generational concentration). Quite a lot is known that points to the existence of distinctive, ranked spheres of exchange in Britain which parallel those described in the last chapter. Marriage and kinship are the strongest channels for exchanged marking services and so of consumption goods. Segregated marriage markets would lead to segregated sharing of very fine distinctions between graded and named consumption types. Such partially segregated marriage markets separate the middle and working classes.[25] Moreover, the working classes make their choice of marriage partners within a smaller local radius.[26] Geographical propinquity is a much less important influence on marital choice in the higher social classes.[27] The measures for social linkage could easily be standardized and used as an index of isolation and poverty.

To continue the borrowing of ideas from international trade, we can suggest one more measure of consumer linkage. It draws upon the fact, noted previously, that the more advanced the economy, the larger its services sector, and its financial and administrative structures. This can be transferred to the case of the individual household by measuring a consumer's information linkage. Expenditure reckoned relevant for this would be any kind of putting-out of administrative work to specialists (the recourse to professional accountants, travel agents, lawyers, stockbrokers, and estate agents), and the direct purchase of specialized advice and teaching (child guidance, career guidance, marriage guidance, medical advice, IQ testing, and lessons in consumption skills, flower-arrangement, skating, music, and swimming). At the household level, size of expenditure on professional information has a close correspondence to size of employment in the tertiary sector of a nation. We should expect to find techniques of exclusion being practiced socially that correspond to professional barriers to entry-guarding occupations in the tertiary sector.

Consumer Technological Linkage

Some examples from English life may help here to illustrate the idea of consumer's linkage. Certain groups of factory workers in Luton were studied by Goldthorpe and Lockwood in 1962.[28] Their report unfolds a tale of social isolation for immigrants who had fairly recently moved down from the Midlands. There was "a variety of evidence to show that for the majority of our affluent workers and their wives time outside work was devoted overwhelmingly to home and family life, rather than to sociability of any more widely-based kinds." Asked to name their two or three most frequent companions, the average for husband and wife together was less than three, and 36 percent of the couples in the sample shared only one or two between them. Asked how they spent their evenings and weekends, the normal answer was that the wife did some housework, the husband went to get cement for the garage floor, the wife shopped, they put up a shelf or laid down linoleum, and they might have been visited by a close relative from up the road. The explanation of this largely privatized style of life given by the authors is not that it is "a sign of incipient middleclassness" but the "adaptation of long-standing working class norms of sociability to new economic and social conditions—those created by mobility and separation from kin, by employment in modern, large-scale plants and by the possibility of attractive housing and high standards of domestic living." They add that the degree of privatization was not

entirely the unwanted and unwelcome consequence of their quest for affluence; . . . the possibility has therefore to be recognised that for some proportion of the couples we studied, being separated from the body of their kin or living in a community in which kinship ties were of slight importance was actually experienced as an advantage in that it made it easier to restrict or to discontinue kinship relations that were found not to be rewarding.[29]

So much for weak social linkage. As to technological linkage:

A majority of workers with whom we were concerned had come to Luton primarily in quest of higher incomes and better living conditions. Moreover, our interviews also suggested that among our sample as a whole the aspirations that were most commonly held for the future were ones relating to steadily increasing consumer capacity and to yet higher material standards of life. In the sphere of domestic consumption at least, there was little evidence at all of any restricting influence being exerted by traditional working class norms. Considering, for example, refrigerators and cars—two high-cost and characteristically 'middle-class' possessions—the extent of ownership proved to be roughly comparable between our manual and non-manual samples. . . . Furthermore, on what might be regarded as the still more revealing matter of house purchase, it emerged that 57% of our affluent workers—compared with 69% of the white collar sample—owned or were buying their present homes." [30]

Here is an example of strong technological linkage, weak social linkage, and indication of some use of information and other services in the equivalent of the tertiary sector, in respect of possible use of house mortgage facilities.

Consumer Social Linkage

As an example of the reverse pattern, take the mining community made famous in sociology by the study of Dennis, Henriques, and Slaughter.[31] This town on the border of the

West Yorkshire coalfields is isolated geographically and much more isolated historically by the specialized nature of its economy. Most of Ashton's men were miners. They shared a clear group identity through their experience of the historic ups and downs of that industry, and through the grave risks to life and limbs and lungs that it notoriously affords. The authors repeatedly aver that at that period coal miners were earning on average above the national industrial wage.[32]

The comparative prosperity of the industry fostered the external boundary, for it enabled them to keep their sons in the industry and to see their daughters married to miners in the town. So the group was self-recruiting and stable in good times. Whenever wages fell, they tended to lose members, but at the time of the research it was in every historical, physical, economic, and demographic sense a self-recruiting, bounded group. They did not all earn at the same wage levels, and the pattern of spending that is recorded implies that household consumption was kept down to the standard of the lower paid. The surplus earnings of the better paid were skimmed off in convivial entertainment of their mates, in betting, and in subscriptions to many charitable and social activities. It was a high-consumption–low-saving economy. This habit was partly explained by the authors by the great insecurities and changes of their employment which make them "give up saving as a bad job, and live from day to day, spending the money as it is earned in the belief that 'they'll manage somehow' come what may." [33] According to Milton Friedman, however (see chapter 2), irregularity of income is the circumstance most favorable to private saving; this case is an exception in that a strong corporate identity does not allow one man to rise above another. If he has more money in his pocket than the others, there are prescribed ways of leveling that inequality and making it a temporary one. The wage structure in Ashton roughly divides the day-wage men, on a fixed and low wage, from the contract men performing different tasks underground and earning much more. In the course of his life a man would normally start on a day-wage, reach the coal face in his late twenties, and retire from it in his fifties. His pattern of household consumption is fixed at the start so that everything he gets over and above day-wage rates is free money, uncommitted and available for his spending on his friends. If this life pattern was everyone's lot, it would still be a question why in the twenty-odd years of high wages they were not expected by the community to improve their homes and invest for a higher standard of consumption, against the inevitable lean years ahead. But the high-earning period of life was not for everyone. In 1953 in the three age-groups—under 25, 26 to 50, and over 50—the following percentages of working men were in highly paid work: 15 percent, 49 percent, 18.5 percent. So even in the best period, 26 to 50 years, just over half the working men were still on the lower wage standard. This, we would argue, plus the demands of solidarity, explains why everyone put aside a modest, basic "wage for the wife" every week and used the surplus for social purposes. Without some such moral as "spend now and be merry, let tomorrow take care of itself," the small community would be divided into economic and social classes. As it is, they could ask scornfully of a man who makes good outside the community, "Why does he give himself airs? He is only a collier like us." If the community were divided, and if the high wage earners were to see their interests as radically different from the others, or if there were any opportunities of making private deals with the management, the loss would be general. (Some alterations in the conditions of work have lately made the unions' representation have a bias towards the contract-wage men, with the predicted bad results for the day-wage men.) The whole organization of their economic life rested on a recognized difference of interest between the employers and the miners, and the latter saw their solidarity as their only strength in driving good wage bargains. In those circumstances it would be fatal to the community to let private success be rewarded by permanent, tangible advantages that could be transmitted to a fortunate few in the next generation. Keeping the level of domestic consumption low all around by draining off the surplus in drink and betting is a way of meeting the basic requirements of a stable group. These miners seemed to watch each other with an eagle eye to notice any deviations from the consumption norms: "Someone produced a rather expensive brand of tobacco. The cry immediately went up, 'My, aren't we posh,' and the middle-aged collier put the tin away in confusion." [34] Surplus cash had to be spent in the approved ways, on public feasting and not on private delectation.

However, there is another aspect of the public feasting which is clearly brought out in the book. The drinking of beer is always shared drinking with friends; it is organized on strict rules of reciprocity. Therefore, if a man is temporarily short of cash, he will accept drinks from a friend, but he will be honor-bound to repay. Ordinarily each stands his turn. Since there is a minority who can afford more than twice as much drink as the others, the simple rule of reciprocity must divide the drinkers into big and smaller leagues, and a man who was once a "big-hitter," when demoted from his contract work team to day-wages, must necessarily move out of the big-drinking league; and likewise for the next stage. When he retires altogether and becomes an old-age pensioner, he can only drink regularly with other old-age pensioners. These distinctions worry the miners, evidently, since providing free drinks on great holidays (eight pints per member at Christmas, Easter, Whitsun, and August Bank Holiday) is one of the charges on those who are earning well. Providing outings and free meals for children and pensioners and contributing to the town bank and the St. John's Ambulance are further levies.

Everything that has been said so far in this account of consumption suggests that heavy outgoing on social relations is not likely to be quite independent of potential revenue. The theoretical position taken at the beginning of this study calls for some connection between social linkage and earning capacity. Here we have observed that the social distinction of belonging to a restricted or a less restricted drinking party corresponds closely to the distinction between high-wage contract team workers and low-wage individuals. The teams at work are self-selecting, and there is competition to get into them and to stay in them. When a man lets down his mates by careless work, illness, or absenteeism, there are others, younger or more stable or stronger, waiting to take his place, and so the team cannot afford to keep him. The work of each team intermeshes with the others. Though their membership is competitive, the various teams with their specialized tasks are interdependent. In this economy there is some very strong competition, but it takes place within the framework of constraints set by the cooperative group. Hence, it would seem, the approval of the hearty drinker and an implicit low value set on private savings. The group will assure that marking services are given, no matter how much they all have to tighten their belts. The researchers strongly got the impression that the women hardly dared complain if they wanted new carpets or better furniture:

A man who gives way to his fiancée or wife is a weakling. A man who is tight with his money when the group are together will not gain prominence or favour with the other members of the group. Miners like a man who says what he thinks in no uncertain manner, shows fear of no-one, and is a liberal spender.[35]

The authors' insensitivity to the women's point of view and their inability to assess women's independence have been questioned subsequently, but the general case of male investment in male social relations connected with work still stands.[36]

This example illustrates strong social linkage through group membership (and evinced by expenditure on convivial occasions) combined with weak technological linkage of the home.

Consumer Information Linkage

It remains to illustrate the last case, in which expenditure is laid out upon shared consumption that will produce for those involved an increase of information. Whether the information thus gained will add to their earning capacity in particular or improve their command over their social universe in general, this is the parallel, in a consumption framework, of outlays upon work search. The costs of seeking information in the labor market have been brought under economists' scrutiny only recently.[37] The theory of perfect competition assumes complete knowledge of the market, yet, where labor is concerned, as Stigler remarks,[38] it costs more to learn of alternative prices than the information yields in rewards. In general, the gains from work search are larger the longer the prospective period of employment, so that those parts of the labor force engaged in short-term, high-turnover occupations are rational in not spending over long in seeking information. The larger the cost of search, the less search will be undertaken by any worker at a given level of dispersion of wage offers. The more specialized the job, the more economical the search. Stigler concludes his important essay by showing that the long-term social return on investment in information is a more efficient allocation of the labor force. The better informed the labor market, the closer each worker's marginal product is to its maximum at any time. Conversely, we may add, blocks in the flow of information are a source of inefficiency. Most of the work in this field has been concentrated, perforce, upon comparing assessed magnitude of returns from search with expenditure upon search, calculated from the cost of not being paid during the period of search. But we need to turn the same spy-glass upon the standing of rounds of beer, the invitations to picnics and parties, the actual consumption of food and drink, of cars and houses and refrigerators—consumption dedicated to multiple and diffuse social purposes, which also yields needful information about the labor market.

John Barnes, in his study of a Norwegian rural community,[39] contrasted the information needs of local farmers and fishermen. The former could manage with a short social network and exhibited few of the worries in this respect that preoccupied the trawler men. These latter, in their highly competitive industry, used the most up-to-date boats and equipment, which they needed to know of promptly and bring quickly from distant places; they also needed to sift and select from the best human material to recruit their crews, often men from hundreds of miles around. Much of their information was gathered informally on the regular picnics and fishing parties they organized in on-shore periods, giving them a very different life-style from the farmers. Dock workers provide another example of the importance of information, in the inverse sense not of gathering, but of emitting information about oneself in the right quarters. Before the days of the unions and decasualization, the individual docker had to take the risk of not being hired and the severe loss it entailed. The men were forced, says David Wilson,[40] to adopt a host of expedients to create unofficial loyalties which aimed at putting one man, and his group, in a position of advantage over the others. Those who had his protection could hope to be called by the foreman; the others, if they belonged to no group, had little chance. Open display of self-interest, however, was imprudent:

Lobbying of the call-stand was driven underground, into the informal network of relationships within the dock community. Rather than jockey in front of the foreman, they relied on private arrangements to improve their chances. This might mean approaching the foreman directly in a pub or getting to know the leader of an established gang in the hope that he would fit you into his team when he had a vacancy; usually most reliance was placed on kinship.

Once again, the prospect of intermarriage rears its head as a prime connection between consumption and employment. (See chapter 4.) In the Manchester docks it was not the casual nature of the work, coming daily to take the lottery of the call, that was responsible for the formation of competing gangs. It lay rather in the organization of dock work:

an experienced gang leader could quickly size up how long it would take to discharge the hold with the equipment available and how much the job would yield in prospect. If he reckoned the yield would be inadequate, he would consult the gang and decide whether to ask for extra pay from the foreman.

If the gang refused the job at the proffered wage, they could be sure that no other dockers would work that hold. The amount of money they claimed never matched the cost of delaying the ship, so agreements were quickly reached. Here is another example of how the organization of work structures the organization of friendship, and therefore of leisure and of patterns of consumption. In the cases both of the dockers and of the miners, the need to be with mates in the pub and to give the expected drinks is important—one of the costs of maintaining a place in the gang. The low level (very often negative) of savings in such a community and Tawney's aphorism about humanity's need to pour wealth away in drink can be assimilated in grid-group analysis.

For the general context of an anthropology of consumption, it is too narrow to treat the costs of information as strictly related to the market for labor. There are political needs for information which even more vitally set the future scope and influence of the individual at a higher level if they can be met. Governments, of course, need information about their rivals, and they pay for it. A rising politician may also have to spend on drink, at a more luxurious level, for the same intrinsic purpose as the dock worker. Badly beset with debts as he was, the young Walpole could not afford to miss his weekly meetings with leading Whigs:

It was at these weekly meetings of the Kit Cat that Walpole learned the arts of convivial politics—if he needed to learn, for no man's temperament was more fitted to take advantage of all the opportunities presented by characters and will enfeebled by drink. Yet, with these men he had no natural advantage, neither birth nor riches. To achieve his mastery over them he had to learn to bridle his too obvious ambition; to check the merited rebuke; to suppress the biting witticism, to learn, in fact, to subjugate his temperament. . . . But these riotous, extravagant evenings, with their abundance of rare food and costly wine, were as valuable to Walpole as long days spent in the Commons.[41]

Political information tends to come this way, in personal contacts at consumption rituals. Hence the watchful rules of inclusion and exclusion. But a determined, ambitious learner of political information cannot but go to the top. In a very different climate and circumstance, we learn of how the Tiv tribe in Nigeria regulate their affairs in an idiom of genealogical descent.

. . . There are a very few Tiv—the politicians and a few scholars at heart—who learn genealogies and other matters to an extent beyond their immediate sphere of daily concerns. Their interest and facility is apart from the common Tiv interest in and use of genealogies. All Tiv live, breathe and talk genealogies, but only in so far as they illustrate some point or relationship. Any distinction between the learning and the use of genealogies is artificial. . . . An adult Tiv gains most of his additional information concerning his dead agnates from the discussion of elders at moots, inquests, funerals and the like. At such events ambitious men of early middle age sit in the background listening closely. The following day one may find them closeted with one of the more knowledgeable elders discussing the fine points of the case. . . . through various comments he acquires a notion of the order of segmentation, of spatial position and of the kind of relationship between them [lineages].

But the farther away in social and geographical space, that is, in the shift from local to national politics, the less sure a Tiv is of the order of segmentation between the larger segments opposable to his own.

Tiv who acquire fuller information do so because their range of interests and activities is wider. Thus one young man of thirty was sent by his father, a government chief, on an errand to a socially and spatially distant lineage, with private instructions to look into current intrigues. He returned with two variants of the internal segmentation of the lineage to which he had been sent—information needed for a thorough grasp of the current political situation, the main purpose of his visit! [42]

Whether the information is sought from formal or informal sources, the parallel with outlays on work search holds good.

The bigger the rewards of information gained, the more expenditure of time and resources is justified in gaining it. But this law is only another example of the cumulative shock mechanism which benefits those who can get benefits of scale. When in the next chapter we divide the population into consumption classes, we shall see that those who spend most on an "information set of goods" are in the most advantaged positions.

Chapter 9

CONSUMPTION
CLASSES

Grouping

In the social structures of less developed countries, it is not difficult to recognize different consumption styles. They usually correspond to very different levels of income, and to a very obvious stratification of society; the big landlords and government classes, then the peasants, and lastly the landless laborers, each circle or layer using its appropriate set of goods. If economists are to succeed in aggregating large numbers of goods into composite commodities, independent of their physical properties, it seems fairly obvious that they would need to look for similar big cleavages in the social structure of developed economies. But here the sociological perception of differences is more ambiguous. Clear-cut patterns of interdining and intermarrying, if they could be discerned, would produce discontinuities in demand. But the sociological analysis fails to reveal such clear-cut patterns, and a fuzzier state of affairs prevails.

Market researchers get around the difficulty, which is a basic one for their advertiser clients, by defining social classes in terms of spending habits and then anchoring this consumption-based definition to occupation and income groupings in a rule-of-thumb way. A conception of a common life-style based on consumption, income, and occupation is a good intuitive assessment of expected life income, which works quite well for their general purposes. Wealth itself is extremely difficult to assess. Occupation categories are no safe guide because they dissolve under inspection into a kaleidoscopic list of components which also points to expected life income.[1] The measured income of any one year is evidently not an important determinant of consumption patterns. In a bad season, people will regard their mutual obligations to give and take marking services as fixed and will borrow to keep up standards, or if they think a good year is going to be exceptional and unrepeated, they do not normally let it greatly alter their consumption routine. For modern industrial society the only reliable way of discovering consumption patterns would be to focus somehow upon the use of goods for social purposes. The consumption criterion used by market researchers could yield a good idea of what social class is like if it were used systematically. But though it could indeed define social class, such a definition of social class could not then be used to explain consumption behavior. Nevertheless, just such a circular explanation of consumer behavior is often heard.

So far there has been no theory of consumption that can relate the varied tastes and activities of the consumer into a single conceptual scheme. But perhaps analysis of the linkage structure (see chapter 8) of consumption behavior would fill some of the theoretical needs. It could confirm that the consumer's rational objective, as here proposed, is to continue to choose rationally in an intelligible world, and that to increase scale of consumption is a rational way of trying to control an expanding information system. It could also reveal the discontinuities in consumption which the class structure of society produces, but which are difficult to uncover by other means. At least we can rehearse here how linkage analysis could be applied to consumers.

Let us consider what would be a telling selection of goods to represent different consumption patterns. Following the model of international trade, we can start by looking for three social categories defined by their consumption of three sets of goods: one, a staples set, corresponding to the primary production sector; the next, a technology set, corresponding to the secondary production sector; and the third, an information set, corresponding to tertiary production. Choosing these terms releases us from the confines of the contrast between necessities and luxuries. This allows us to look beyond necessities (defined by income-responsiveness) for the appropriate defining types of consumption for each social class. In the first case for the social class defined by a staples set, food is the obvious defining expenditure. These households will be identified by Engel's law, according to which a higher proportion of total expenditure goes to food than to other goods. The other two social classes are already defined in that food takes a declining proportion of the total. But it would be a mistake to look for some other set of goods, the demand for which behaves like the demand for food, to define the consumption of the other two social classes. As long as the demands for the various goods that we expect to aggregate all move together, it makes sense for those goods to be treated as one composite commodity. There is no reason for requiring that the demand for it behaves in the same way as demand for goods in another set. Rather, the reverse: since we are looking for separate divisions within a complex social system, the divisions will be organically related and most unlikely therefore to replicate each other's structure. So we expect a secondary consumption class to be distinguished by a high income elasticity for travel and consumer's capital equipment. Given the definition of the staples class, there will here be scope for a relatively higher proportion of expenditure on the defining goods of the technology set.

By dropping the term "luxuries," we have fortunately lost the moral slur and also the heterogeneity in the concept of nonstaple consumption. A category of "information" goods is not vacuous, nor is such expenditure frivolous or immoral. Just as sweet biscuits, however harmful, must be classified with food, so must theater and concert tickets and pornographic literature count as information. Education is a serious matter, even if the category has to include payment for all kinds of lessons, classes in bronze-casting, charm, or Spanish dancing. However mixed, these can be acceptably placed under the logical umbrella of buying information. (Later we shall need to distinguish formal from informal sources of information.) By definition—and for the same reasons as the technology set —the information set would define a class of consumption with a lower income elasticity for food and a lesser proportion of income spent upon it. It would have a high income elasticity for technology, but not necessarily a higher proportion of income spent on it. At almost any income level conflict can be seen between buying a new consumer durable, or even a new house, and maintaining a given standard of information services, a conflict which in this social class by definition will be settled by preferring information over technology. The defining feature of this class is the relatively higher proportion of expenditure that goes toward buying information.

We are here suggesting three distinctive consumption patterns:

1. small scale, defined by high proportion of total expenditure on food;
2. medium scale, defined by a relatively higher proportion of total expenditure on the set of goods currently representing advanced consumer technology, and a high income elasticity for this set, combined with a relatively declining proportion of total expenditure on and lower income elasticity for food;

3. large scale, defined by a relatively higher proportion of expenditure on information (formal and informal), combined with a high income elasticity for the technology set, and a lower income elasticity and lesser proportion of income spent on food.

Admission to the Top Class

Since the smallest scale of consumption is obviously income constrained and the expenditure pattern well known, interest turns to the other two consumption patterns. If they exist at all in a distinguishable way is the first thing to examine; the next important question is whether they are determined by different positions on the scale of income distribution. If income and family size alone determine consumption patterns, then, since the line of income distribution is very smooth in Britain, there should be no sharp breaks in consumption habits and no distinctive consumption patterns to be revealed. The shift from small to large scale should be indiscernibly gradual and blurred. By the same argument, the society of Britain would be more or less classless, the main distinctions in consumption patterns being traceable to family size or to differences in earning power, especially to the long-term difference due to employment or unemployment of the household head. The anthropological argument goes the other way: it would be rational for every individual household to tend toward a large-scale consumption pattern, but not all will achieve it, and the obstacles are not only a matter of income. There may seem to be no intrinsic reason why, through the whole society, all households should not be spending roughly the same proportions of income on information goods and services. But there is one reason: ethnography suggests that competition to acquire goods in the information class will generate high admission barriers and efficient techniques of exclusion. Ethnography suggests that, left to themselves, regardless of how evenly access to the physical means of production may be distributed, and regardless of free educational opportunities, consumers will tend to create exclusive inner circles controlling access to a certain kind of information.

Earlier, when writing about the tertiary sector in production, we took a positive line and argued as if it were obvious that the provision of administrative, financial, and brokerage services were a form of social overhead, a necessary condition of economic development as much as roads and railways, and the means of expanding the scale of production. But, of course, the matter is more controversial. The tertiary sector has come in for the same disparagement in international economics as have luxuries in writing on consumption. The services sector may indeed deserve the abuse it gets, as a parasitic clerical class battening on the honest labors of the poor. Likewise, luxuries, in the true pejorative sense, can suck away the product of the majority's labor for the private delectation of an exclusive elite, who give very little back to the rest of the economy and are mainly interested in preserving their hegemony. The picture has to be carefully analyzed. We are interested precisely in the use of consumption goods to control information; the general run of the argument does not imply that the uses of the information set of goods are always either neutral or beneficial and never harmful.

Two points will establish why the top consumption class is worth gaining admission to. First, it obtains a higher rate of earnings than the others, and second, competence in judging information goods and services is a qualification for employment in that better paid sector. These two points, resulting in a feedback from consumption to employment, would suffice to establish the circular process linking consumption with earnings in the economy as a whole. The first surely needs no emphasis. It is almost tautologous. The earning potential of persons spreading their consumption over a large proportion of the information set of goods is better than that of the rest of the population. The big spenders in the information set are themselves the big producers of the information goods. This is a crucially important point, which we will return to in the next chapter. At some time in his life, anyone may need the services of a solicitor or clergyman, for most marry, inherit, bequeath, and all die. Most will have resorted to doctors and hospitals, and enjoyed spectator sports, concerts, or the theater. The whole public uses the information-producing sector. But within each branch of information there is a professional training of the ear and eye to catch new wisps of information that will give a competitive edge to the service offered, and specialized information-brokerage institutions serving the need for the best information. A would-be playwright sees more plays than other people, a would-be conductor goes to more concerts and buys more records, the writer buys more books. So though they skim their income off a large market, they themselves indulge their own highly discriminated forms of enjoyment—as their larger earnings allow them to do. Furthermore, there is likely to be more interdining and intermarriage among the producers of the various information services just because they are in a similar income bracket. Willmott and Young's survey of leisure activities in Great Britain shows a much stronger tendency for there to be some link between work and leisure in the top social class—39 percent of the professional and managerial class in the sample—but much lower in the other social classes.

Though it seems likely that the top consumption class tends to segregate itself in its leisure activities, its demand for even very spiritual pleasures, for nonmaterial things like opera or fresh air, sets off a demand for material adjuncts like opera houses or yachting marinas. Being richer, they lead demand, and their leadership endows all other activities with value according to a hierarchy graded by their intentions. Their switches in fashion change the price structure all down the line, and their preferences have the power to be self-sustaining. This leads to the second point, that competence in judging information goods is a qualification for higher income.

The contention is that entry into the services sector of the productive system is made easier by prior entry into the social class that consumes the information set of goods. This corresponds to another aspect of the tertiary sector in international trade. This sector, though it uses highly specialized skills (such as financial and legal expertise), also gives employment to quite unskilled workers in domestic or brokerage services. Sabolo has shown that this gives the services sector a capacity to absorb and pay relatively better an unskilled rural population made surplus to a more capital intensive agriculture.[2] Similarly, many who gain employment in producing information services do not need long training or specialized skills. But it would help if they had a well-trained ear or eye or palate or some other consumption expertise. Linder [3] observed and demonstrated that the richest countries tended to trade together most, and those with the most similar structure of demand did more trade with each other than with the rest. He explained this by the advantages in understanding the market that comes from a home-based demand for the same kind of goods. That case can be made even more clearly and strongly for the advantages in gaining employment for the individual who wants to be highly paid, who can see that earnings are high in the services sector, and whose private consumption habits have trained him in an immensely fine judgment of names in some part of the range of valued information goods and services.

The analysis that follows pays special attention to finding the break between the small-scale and the large-scale consumption classes predicted above, so as to justify these interesting analogies between the tertiary sector of employment in the nation and the information set of consumption goods in the household.

Linkage Tests

The tabulations that follow seek evidence from the 1973 Family Expenditure Survey [4] of consumption classes such as those just discussed. They are arranged by occupation of household head: the effects of family composition and size have been taken into account; the information about weekly income is net of taxes and includes in it the earnings of all members of the household. Table 9–1–A shows how the numbers of each composite occupational category in the sample are spread through different "equivalent" income groups: only 63 households of the top class (professional and technical workers, administrative and managerial workers, and teachers) are in the lowest income group, that is the lowest 20 percent of the equivalent income distribution; the majority are in the top income group. Of course their range of incomes extends beyond the division of the top quintile point (£51 per week), the average of the top 20 percent being about £80 per week. With manual unskilled workers, the clustering is the other way, with a small minority in the top income group; the same is true for the retired and the unoccupied.

Three kinds of goods have been selected to indicate expenditure that seems to correspond reasonably well to linkage types. Informal information sources constitute social linkage which is judged here on whether the household spends on its own telephone account; formal information linkage depends on whether it pays for the advantage of a bank account; and technological linkage on whether it runs a car and so spends on gas and oil.

These items have been chosen after examining the material basis of the culture. In the same spirit Derek Stenning reckoned how many cows a Fulani herdsman would need to keep his wives and children supplied with milk; how many wives he should have performing dairying duties so as to strike the right balance between the human and animal population; and how many cows he would need to pay his annual tribute for grazing rights, settle certain, foreseeable debts, marry his sons, and hold up his head as an independent man.[5] For the present exercise, we take ownership of a car to indicate the technological capacity of the household. Richer families may go for a quality car or for several cars, and there will be a difference between urban and rural habits in respect to cars. By itself, lack of a car is not significant, and it is very possible that car ownership is not the best item to take for this purpose. In itself, to be discovered without a car means nothing, but the assumption underlying this linkage test is that to be discovered without a car and without either telephone or bank account will fairly signal a small-scale consumption pattern. For readers who may suppose that car ownership is a very general thing, too general to indicate anything about control of the technology of private transportation, it is worth noting that in industrial Lancashire, in a 1966 sample census, there were fewer than forty cars per hundred households, in the suburban belt of Cheshire, seventy-five, and over ninety in Hale, Bowden, Wilmslow, and Macclesfield. In the "best" of the suburbs, 20 percent of the families had two cars.[6]

Ownership of a bank account is taken to indicate a minimum payment for professional information and services. In richer households, stronger information linkage (represented here minimally by bank charges) will balloon out into a wide array of specialist advisory and administrative services. A household using none of these is like a less developed country in respect of its administrative and financial sectors. The installation of a telephone in the home will be an indication of some social linkage, even though in many cases it is needed for self-employed businesses. There are other snags about this set: since the custom of paying wages by checks is occupationally linked, the bank account in itself is not so significant, no more than is the car taken by itself. There are also households, not enumerated, which recorded one or two but not all three of these types of expenditure. Table 9–2 shows households with very weak consumer linkage and therefore, in our terms, small-scale consumption: these households, 30 percent of all households, spent on none of the test items. The occupational groups are ranged according to income range, and so according

TABLE 9-1
Consumers' Linkage Tests

Occupation—First Adult	Equivalent* Normal† Net‡ Household § Income (£ percents)					Total
	Lowest 20	Second 20	Middle 20	Fourth 20	Top 20	

A. Distribution of Households

Occupation—First Adult	Lowest 20	Second 20	Middle 20	Fourth 20	Top 20	Total
Professional and technical workers, administrative and managerial workers, teachers	63	115	183	349	663	1373
Clerical workers and shop assistants	30	69	105	131	119	454
Manual workers—skilled and semiskilled	288	578	736	656	393	2651
Manual workers—unskilled	75	112	92	61	29	369
Retired and unoccupied	879	457	214	135	126	1811
All households**	1340	1339	1339	1339	1338	6695

SOURCE: Compiled by analysis of data from Department of Employment, *Family Expenditure Survey, 1973* (HMSO, 1974).

*Family composition made equivalent.

**Including households with first adult in armed forces.

†*Normal*—several weeks running.

‡Net of income taxes and National Insurance Contributions.

§ Aggregate income for all individuals in household.

B. Average Equivalent Normal Net Household Income (£ per week)

Occupation—First Adult	Lowest 20	Second 20	Middle 20	Fourth 20	Top 20	Total
Professional and technical workers, administrative and managerial workers, teachers	18.34	28.06	35.27	45.00	80.67	58.29
Clerical workers and shop assistants	20.26	27.78	35.95	44.40	62.78	43.14
Manual workers—skilled and semiskilled	20.70	28.01	35.24	44.56	63.33	38.55
Manual workers—unskilled	19.78	27.59	35.15	43.88	60.31	33.15
Retired and unoccupied	19.66	27.13	34.80	43.70	72.62	39.97
All households	19.84	27.67	35.23	44.54	72.63	39.97

SOURCE: Compiled by analysis of data from Department of Employment, *Family Expenditure Survey, 1973* (HMSO, 1974).

TABLE 9-1 (continued)

	Equivalent Normal Net Household Income (£ percents)					
Occupation—First Adult	Lowest 20	Second 20	Middle 20	Fourth 20	Top 20	Total
	C. Age of Head of Household (Years)					
...ofessional and technical ...orkers, administrative and ...anagerial workers, teachers	39.6	39.7	38.8	41.1	44.5	42.2
...rical workers and shop ...istants	45.7	43.0	44.8	46.6	48.0	45.9
...nual workers—skilled and ...niskilled	41.9	42.7	43.3	45.1	43.4	43.5
...nual workers—unskilled	49.7	47.8	51.3	50.8	49.9	49.7
...tired and unoccupied	67.7	69.1	67.5	68.1	66.3	67.9
...households	59.2	51.8	47.1	46.8	46.6	50.3

SOURCE: Compiled by analysis of data from Department of Employment, *Family Ex-diture Survey, 1973* (HMSO, 1974).

to expected permanent income. Descending that scale, the figure of households without telephone, bank account, or car increases regularly, from 5.3 percent of the professional group sample to 55.6 percent of the retired and unoccupied.

Table 9–3 turns the picture around by showing the percentage of all households recording expenditure on all three test items. The figure of 12.4 percent of the total population is surprisingly low and suggests that the test is a searching one. Note that there is a big jump between the category of clerical workers and shop assistants (19.8 percent) spending on all three items, and the skilled and semiskilled manual workers (only 8.9 percent), a divergence that is found at each income level for these occupations. It is also noticeable that in the top incomes of the clerical workers' group, the proportion spending on all three test items is similar to the proportion spending on all three in the professional group, taken as a whole. So evidently the clerical workers have the same idea

TABLE 9-2
Ownership Levels: Negative

Percentage of Households Recording No Expenditure on Own Telephone Account, Bank Charges, Gas and Oil

Occupation—First Adult	Equivalent Normal Net Household Income (£ percents)					Total (percentage
	Lowest 20	Second 20	Middle 20	Fourth 20	Top 20	
Professional and technical workers, administrative and managerial workers, teachers	14.3	15.7	10.4	4.6	1.7	5.3
Clerical workers and shop assistants	40.0	31.9	22.9	13.0	6.7	18.3
Manual workers—skilled and semiskilled	47.2	35.3	27.0	16.9	11.7	26.3
Manual workers—unskilled	62.7	53.6	55.4	37.7	24.1	51.0
Retired and unoccupied	75.3	52.3	31.8	19.3	8.7	55.6
All households	64.9	40.7	27.0	14.5	6.3	30.7

SOURCE: Compiled by analysis of data from Department of Employment, *Family Expenditure Surveys, 1973* (HMSO, 1974).

about the kind of consumption pattern they are aiming at, and only income holds them back. (This supports our argument that consumers' objectives can be formulated in these general terms.) But it is not income which separates their consumption pattern from that of the skilled manual workers. The range of expected life income is very similar, so that neither wealth nor measured income differences explain the divergence. Here we have the basis of a divergence between consumption patterns, the evidence for a consumption-defined class system that rests upon scale of consumption as we have been developing the notion.

Several other ways of probing in this area would be worth

TABLE 9-3
Ownership Levels: Positive

*Percentage of Households Recording Expenditure on Own
Telephone Account, Bank Charges, Gas, and Oil*

Occupation—First Adult	Equivalent Normal Net Household Income (£ percents)					Total (percentage)
	Lowest 20	Second 20	Middle 20	Fourth 20	Top 20	
ofessional and technical rkers, administrative and anagerial workers, teachers	12.7	22.6	29.0	33.8	33.9	30.8
erical workers and shop istants	6.7	11.6	15.2	22.1	29.4	19.8
anual workers—skilled and niskilled	4.2	5.0	7.1	12.4	15.5	8.9
anual workers—unskilled	0	2.7	5.4	4.9	10.3	3.8
tired and unoccupied	0.5	1.5	4.7	11.1	19.1	3.3
households	2.0	5.5	10.2	18.5	25.8	12.4

SOURCE: Compiled by analysis of data from Department of Employment, *Family Expenditure Survey*, 1973 (HMSO, 1974).

trying. For example, if bank charges could be combined with any other types of information expenditure, oil and fuel expenditure with total expenditure on private transport, and if actual private telephone expenditures could be recorded instead of just the bare fact of paying rental for a telephone, the streaming of consumption according to well-scaled patterns ought to emerge more clearly.

Then again, it would be interesting to choose items for the three branches that would reveal another more exclusive class within the 12.4 percent who use all three of the first set of test items. Perhaps for technology the ownership of more than one home would be telling. Expenditure on housing and furnishing is notoriously difficult to compare cross-culturally, since subsidized housing varies, as do the proportions of house ownership and rented accommodation, and there are also different facilities for mortgaging, leasing, and so on. In general the poor have a low-income elasticity and a high proportion of expenditure on housing or rent. But for the rich, housing is not a necessity in terms of income-responsiveness. The subject bristles with technicalities, but Dr. Margaret Reid has spent great statistical ingenuity in unraveling the figures about United States expenditure on housing, tracking errors, and allowing for the effects of normal income. She says that "for the US elasticity of housing with respect to normal income may be as high as 2. This suggests to me that high quality housing may, in fact, be one of the important luxuries of our economy, a principal consumption item distinguishing the rich from the poor." [7] Thus she supports Marshall's observation that "relatively large and well-appointed house room is, even in the lowest social ranks, at once a 'necessary for efficiency' and the most convenient and obvious way of advancing a material claim to social distinction." [8] In the present argument the reason for this will be that housing is used for social linkage and the rich tend to buy more of it, as much of it as they can. If we decide that housing belongs with capital and technology, what about a test item for social linkage for the top consumption class?

Because of the exclusiveness that is postulated for this consumption class, a good test would be a form of expenditure on the learned fine arts, opera, for example, or pictures, or on straight collecting—coins, incunabula, old music scores, old porcelain, old glass, or other objects that carry an immensely technical and deep-stacked hierarchy of names which only the devoted connoisseur could master, and which have no intrinsic usefulness. But this would have to be the subject of a special survey, for there are too few members of this class in the Family Expenditure Survey population. As to information linkage, probably expenditure on private education would usefully close the brackets on a class of top consumers.

By such means we could expect to find a division between the lower and upper parts of our society in terms of ownership levels of a consumer-linkage package comprising telephone, bank, and car. Within the upper class we would expect to divide it again according to expenditure levels on housing, fine arts, and education. But year by year the linkage tests would need to be revised to discover the real divisions within society.

There might be another way of identifying this last top class. From small- to large-scale consumption patterns, the relative expenditures on the class-defining goods tend to rise, but absolute proportions on each set of goods would probably tend to become more alike. A measure of difference of absolute proportions spent on selected categories of goods might prove an interesting index of social class. It sounds perhaps farfetched. But there is some reason to suppose that the large-scale consumption pattern is characterized by a very wide spread among types of activity. An analogy with dietary habits may illustrate the point. At the poor man's table a cheap carbohydrate staple predominates at every meal. At a higher income level there will still be a recognizable staple food in the diet, but there will be more variety. At a still higher level it will be hard to say what the staple is; bread, potato, beans, lentils take their turn with meat, fish, and legumes in continual variety. Similarly, it is possible that in the top consumption class it is less easy to say what is the largest item of expenditure.

This measure of difference of absolute proportions spent may be a way of presenting information about different life-styles that other statistical data fail to capture. It is building on the well-known increase in variety that is practically synonymous with increase in real income, recognized by Jevons and Marshall in the following quotations:

there soon arise the greater variety and elegance in dress; and to this succeeds the desire to build, to ornament and to furnish—tastes which seem to increase with every improvement in civilization.[9]

There is a constant increase both in that variety and expensiveness which custom requires as a minimum, and in that which it tolerates as a maximum, and the efforts to obtain distinction by dress are extending themselves throughout the lower grades of English society.[10]

Time

It still has to be shown that the linkage test based on goods is really a measure of social involvement, to such a degree that the social relationships maintained by the shared consumption can be expected to have a good effect on earning capacity.

There is a strong presumption that a private telephone is not entirely used for business, or for ordering household goods and making complaints or appointments with the gas fitters and plumbers. But we must admit that private use of the telephone and postal services is not necessarily all traffic in marking services. The telephoning and letter-writing may count more as time-saving facilities for seeking out and ordering consumption goods and paying for them. If this is the main use of the private telephone, it suggests that the time factor is more valuable for one consumption group, for getting food, technology, and information, and for keeping in touch with fellow consumers. One part of the expenditure on postal services and the telephone should strictly count as information linkage, paying for putting out of the household the costs of administration; the other part is then used for true marking services—calls to friends, inquiries after sickness, invitations, personal news, and so on. According to the General Post Office's own consumer surveys,[11] British telephone users are generally better educated, earn higher incomes, already possess a television and a car, and are younger than that part of the market which this service has not yet reached. They use the telephone not only for business, but also for conversing with family and friends, for household affairs, and voluntary work. We are moving toward an explanation of the slow spread of telephones in the United Kingdom compared with television.

Consumption Classes

All that expenditure on telephoning and letter-writing would be a straight effect of education, and itself an indicator of life income. The young professionals might as well save on kitchen equipment and get their telephone installed at once since everyone they know and expect to know is wired up to one. But why don't all those others want to save that time? And why don't they feel unduly cut off from their friends if they fail to install a telephone? Note that as late as 1972, the proportion of potential telephones to total households in the United Kingdom was only about 40 percent, and that the most complete penetration was clustered around the top of the economic and social scale.

Figure 9–1 illustrates the contrast between the expenditure on the telephone service and expenditure on television. Television, though it transmits information, does not enter into the exchange of marking services, so expenditure on it would only count as small-scale consumption.

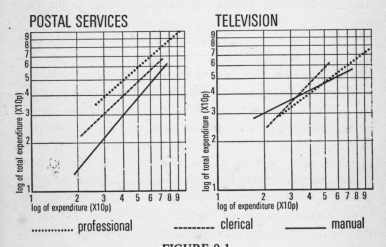

FIGURE 9-1

Engel Curves for Two Service Components

From *Family Expenditures Survey*, HMSO, 1974.

At every income level the professional classes spent more on postal services than the other two occupational groups, though their income elasticity, evidenced by the slope of the curve, was very similar. The manual class shows a smaller proportion of expenditure on postal services and a slightly more steeply sloping elasticity, but when it comes to television it has a distinctly flatter elasticity of income curve, television having become the common commodity we know it to be.

Figure 9–1 sums up something about the use of time and its value in different consumption classes. It seems that the poor always have time on their hands, and less things to do with it than the rich.

Chapter 10

CONTROL OF VALUE

Perhaps we should now consider Maurice Halbwachs's idea that the uses of time could provide defining criteria of social class. "Peut-être la capacité de prévoir ainsi pour l'année les grandes catégories de dépense n'est-elle point elle-même en réalité un moyen de les distinguer."

In the course of this essay, moving toward a differentiated idea of time associated with different kinds of consumption activity, we have tried to draw attention to the importance of periodicity and synchronization of responsibilities. Halbwach's theory that the condition of their lives inhibits the poor from taking a long view is consistent with Oscar Lewis's association of a pancultural, short time scale with poverty. We have also suggested that incorporation in a group lengthens the time span of decisions immeasurably, since a group expects to go on forever. By its very expectation, it can validate its time scale, since it causes funds to be streamed towards a distant future and so enables its expectation to be made actual. In discussing time, then, we have to take account of the self-fulfilling character of a short- or long-term view. The short view expects a curtain of uncertainty to foreclose on its longer-term decisions, but the very fact of everyone taking a short view creates that uncertainty which justifies their concern. The long-term view is self-fulfilling in the parallel way, as long as resources are channeled to the ends it foresees. If we made a list of all the generative tendencies that distinguish two consumption patterns of different scale, the self-fulfilling character of expectations about time would be one of the most significant. The result is that where there is a section of society which is only tentatively and sporadically engaged in the main productive system, time will always hang on its hands. A curious survey of the amount of rest taken in the day in Belgian and Peruvian offices showed an inverse correlation between resting and education,[1] as one would expect, but this does not imply that the more educated have the best ideas about how to occupy themselves. The same source quotes a sociological report on Sicily: "Their life is threaded through by poverty, sickness and despair, but rarely do they lack time for leisure," and another on the life-style of Indian peasants in Peru: "Time losses are thus a heritage." The fact of not being fully involved in the process of production explains the large amount of time hanging heavily on the poor, and this despite all the high-frequency household processing that might be thought to keep them busy. But it can also be argued that their not being heavily involved in consumption processes also gives them more time: this occurs because low involvement reduces the standards at which they expect to furnish their homes, polish the furniture, change their clothes, and serve their meals; and also because a small-scale social round is anyway less time-consuming. Staffen Linder notes that the so-called leisure classes are rushing around hectically trying to put more and more real consumption into a nearly fixed time slot. He is satisfied to explain it by the fact that productivity of working time is vastly increased while consumption time has hardly changed.[2] This sort of explanation depends on the idea of an irrational consumer, to whom the economist cannot resist preaching a change of heart.

Much nearer the mark is Hirschmann's explanation. Bewildered at why he ever got talked into finding time to travel, to consume food and drink and to speak at one more symposium, he disagrees with engaging frankness with Linder. Quoting Hobbes: "All men naturally strive for honour and preferment, but chiefly they who are least troubled with caring for necessary things," Hirschmann confesses his belief that the uneven experience of time between social classes is due to a universal high income elasticity for "obituary-improving activities." [3] The difference that we are trying to establish between the information branch and the other branches of consumption is that honor and preferment are to be had in the information branch, therefore the competition for them is fierce. That would be one reason why consumption is so much more elaborate and tension-ridden at this end of the social system, and why attention to marking services, when so much hangs upon them being given in the standardized way, is time-consuming in itself. But there are other reasons for the pressure upon time in these privileged classes, reasons that emerge when we look more closely at the relevant information and see how it is generated and escapes from control.

Once again an insight from international trade analysis is very suggestive. It is a feature of the tertiary, or services sector, that it calls for relatively little support from capital investment. It also has scope for employing a relatively untrained labor force. This means that a strongly developed tertiary sector is a potential source of innovation, since there is no heavy investment tied up in capital equipment which would have to be discounted if a radical change were contemplated. It follows, too, that the market for information is going to be both competitive and unstable. There is bound to be some demand, even in the most benighted bureaucracy, for cost-reducing innovations on the part of administration and finance, so the larger the tertiary sector, the better endowed we would expect research to be, whether it is biased toward copying, talent-spotting, industrial espionage, or pure research with no specific payoff in view. In this sector one can identify the reallocative ability of the whole economy, for here the main production of new ideas is going on. To reallocative ability Linder credits the main source of comparative advantage in international trade. There is a continual disturbance of the information, due to the search for economies, and a continual disturbance (accumulation and destruction) of information, due to the funding of research.

The creative arts are also part of this sector. When there is a very competitive market for the marking services they provide, there will be a premium on originality and artistic creativity. Any newcomer who wants to break through into big earnings, say as a playwright, ballet dancer, or writer, will have to challenge the supremacy of the established set of names in his field and replace it with a newly fashionable set. There will be a constantly renewed reflection upon society and the human lot, again disturbing to the value of the total stock of information that any one person can hold or survey. Most art critics are sensitive to these switches of judgment. To illustrate the point, we refer to Calvin Tomkins's study aptly entitled *Ahead of the Game: Four Versions of the Avant-Garde,* in which the concern to be new, to break through existing barriers, to mark a turning point is explicitly exemplified and linked to changes in science and technology.[4] Grid-group analysis of nonindustrial cultures suggests that fashion-switching syncretism is not characteristic of industrial societies alone but is associated with low-grid social environments. In these circumstances the problem of controlling or disseminating information is made more difficult by continual change in the stock of information itself. When the whole environment is one in which inventiveness is being encouraged and paid for, there will be a great sense of shortage of time.[5] It is not just a matter of rushing to catch and use a particular form of marking, while the season for it is on, though that may matter, too. In the top consumption class the attempts of some to control the information scene are being foiled by others who stand to gain by changing it. But since this is the class that both uses and fabricates the information, naturally they cannot help but outbid each other and speed up the game, turning the society into a more and more individualistic and competitive scene. As they do so, something quite simple happens which increases the differences between their class and those at the bottom.

The problem concerns transmission of information through barriers of varying thickness. Simon and Ando use an example from thermodynamics to illustrate a relevant feature of dynamic systems.[6] They take the case of a house, completely insulated from the outside weather, with various partitions inside. In each room is placed a thermometer that records the time it takes for a centrally placed stove to bring all the rooms up to the same temperature. The time taken to permeate the partitions tells us about the internal insulating structure of the house. The time record itself can be used to measure the strength of the partitions. This is a study that has influenced our approach to consumption. We have gone around the consumption behavior of a nation with batches of thermometers, as it were, placing them in obvious places to try to find partitions and assess their insulating strength. We have taken the interhousehold economic behavior and treated it as a subsystem of the international economy. Making free with the assumption that the macrosystem, if it is stable, can be decomposed into a stable set of subsystems, we have found it very worthwhile to assume that the major productive sectors of a national economy correspond in some way to major consumption classes. It is a basic assumption of economics that the productive system is ultimately structured the way it is in response to decisions about allocation of resources made in households.

It is reasonable to seek in the systemic character of those decisions a common structure that holds between households and the wider national economy. The concept of marking services introduces a firm connection between the scale of production and the scale of consumption. The household is engaged in producing and exchanging marking services. By examining the frequency of various activities in the household production process, and by reducing the problems of seeking and controlling information to problems of synchronizing periodicities, the existing state of technology plays its proper part in defining the direct relationship between household and national production processes. The subsystem of exchanging households is like a set of partitioned rooms within the nation. The partitioning is made and revealed by the different periodicities that separate the top from the middle and the middle from the lowest and largest part of the population. Household, nation, and the international economy can be nested in a single giant stack because the root principles of the most inclusive system are the same as those governing the household system. International trade itself is a response to demand originating in the individual household's quest for larger scale. So far, the house analogy of Simon and Ando works well. But their main interest required them to suppose that their house was efficiently insulated from outside, and this would be quite wrong for the system we are describing. As it is not externally insulated, heat loss from many interesting causes needs to be taken into account. If we adapt the metaphor in this one respect, we can explain why the difference in temperature between the top and the bottom of the house is so difficult to reduce.

Starting with our three consumption classes, let one be the ground floor, one the middle, and one the top of a house that is divided into many rooms by vertical partitions that are thinner than the flooring. But suppose that, unlike the Simon and Ando house, the roof gives poor insulation, and suppose that the source of the heat is located somewhere on the top floor. Of course, it takes time to warm through the thin partitions between all the top rooms, and then to heat the thick horizontal partition so that the warmth reaches the middle, and more time still to reach the ground floor. Depending on the rate at which the heat is escaping through the roof, and on the heat-resisting thickness of the floors, the bottom floor may never get heated at all. Explaining the parable, the loss of heat corresponds to continual destruction of some information and introduction of new combinations and new ideas, fads, and shifts of interest. It could result from a limited social instability that would correspond to the case which A. B. Atkinson makes concerning the distribution of wealth in modern Britain. The degree of concentration of wealth here is, he argues,

higher than in other industrial countries such as the United States. There has been some decline over the course of this century in the degree of inequality, but there are reasons for believing that this reflects the rearrangement of wealth within families rather than distribution between rich and poor.[7]

He cites various cumulative advantages that accrue to wealth-holders and concentrates on the legislation that might weaken their exclusive control. Legislation can do a lot, but the problem is more general. To apply our house metaphor, the people on the top floor are evidently feeling cold and noticing the drafts. They are concentrating their energies on keeping a warm corner for their own families while others experiment with curing the draft by switching off the heat in one room and switching it on in another. Never feeling warm enough, they spend more energy on insulating the floor with thicker carpets. We know why they feel so cold. The thermal metaphor is all wrong. They are not cold; they are worried about their power to endow goods, persons, places, and times with value. They are worried about the world as they know it, and they have plenty of reason to worry. It is bound to change.

Anthropology is not the discipline for finding solutions to problems. Its homespun common sense is rarely comforting. Various precedents suggest that the best way not to be worried by power and its trappings is to opt right out of the competition; that means going alone into the desert or forming a commune with high walls around it—a hard choice. However, anthropology is perhaps a good discipline for expressing particular social problems in the most general terms.

We have used anthropology to justify the rejection of the materialist approach to consumption, since it creates more problems than it solves. Goods are now to be seen as the medium, less objects of desire than threads of a veil that disguises the social relations under it. Attention is directed to the flow of exchanges, the goods only marking out the pattern.

Where the argument leads is hard to see. To pause here, at a loss, is to pause in good company. The move from utility theory to empirical analyses of international trading patterns has put the argument about the uses of goods into a much more interesting light. But the economists working there are themselves pausing and looking around for better theoretical schemes.

Concentrating on comparative advantage in advanced technological control is not in itself a breakaway from the traditional analysis of international trade. It just means adding technological know-how to the old list of factor endowments. Nathan Rosenberg has suggested that in a world where rapid technological change is taking place, we may need an analytic apparatus that focuses in a central way upon the process of technological change itself, and that we can no longer treat it as an exogenous force that leads to disturbance of equilibrium situations and thereby sets in motion an adjustment process leading to a new equilibrium. We should then give

a more prominent role to the effects of a dynamic technology on comparative advantage . . . the continually changing result of human ingenuity and inventiveness, reflecting the differential capacity of different countries to *develop* techniques which enable them to take advantage of opportunities that are only implicit in their resource endowment . . . the primacy of resource endowment recedes as an explanatory variable in a country's economic opportunities. . . .[8]

This differential ability of countries to produce technical change is not incorporated into theories about international trade. We should inquire, he says, into the sources of technological versatility. If it can be established that certain kinds of economic activities are more successful than others in contributing to the development of inventive abilities and entrepreneurial and organizational talents, there would be important policy implications.

As well as thinking of how to deploy existing resources, we should incorporate into the model the as yet nonexistent resources which will be at the nation's disposal in the future. To bring all these into being, to give human inventiveness its full scope, that badly insulated, badly heated house would have to be reconditioned. The vision of free and equal trading partners in an international society, with the gap between rich and poor nations narrowing and closing, is wrecked if the vast majority of the people of each nation passively receive information and are not actively involved in "assigning probabilities and pay-offs to alternative views of the future." The inhabitants of the top floor would have to be reassured, promised a new heating engineer who can redesign a place where everyone can be warm, so there could be an end to the extra carpets and an end to elbowing to a place near the fire. For it is their behavior that is controlling the rate of change, and extending the distance between poor and rich. They are shortening everyone's time perspective for the sake of their own competitive anxiety, generating waste while at the same time deploring it. What is needed is a design that would change the mood of anxiety on the top floor, so that they could even enjoy the vision of a world moving out of their own control. Such a design will require much deliberation.

The next steps which should follow from this argument are in philosophy, in econometrics and in sociology. Economics takes its problems first as they arise politically, seeks technical means for stating them and solving them, and then develops new, specialized problems from the nature of the technical apparatus it has devised. Given this sphere of expertise, it accepts its fundamental assumptions from other disciplines and gives them back as problems. The concept of economic rationality is a philosophical problem. The econometrician will find different ways of working out his predictions if provided with a concept of rationality which takes account of the rational being's first need to interpret the world as intelligible. In this book we have tried to show why that is necessary and some of what changes in thinking it would involve. We have also tried to produce a tool, still clumsy but suggestive, which would uncover the deep discontinuities in social class which are disguised to the economist's eye by the smooth gradation of the income distribution across all social classes. Most important support for this line of thinking could come from sociologists taking seriously the concept of separate marriage markets and distinctive patterns of dissociation from those who marry across the boundaries. Undoubtedly there are gaps in social involvement which leave some households isolated and economically vulnerable. These gaps are not the result of particular capitalist production processes. We find them in other kinds of society. They arise from decisions not to share consumption rituals, not to invite to the home. They mark the boundaries of sharing and hospitality. Innumerable free, private decisions to exclude result in distinctive consumption patterns and segregated marriage markets. When the in-marrying of privilege and wealth happens in India or Africa, we can detect it very easily. When it happens at home we cannot perceive it. As a result, the problem of poverty in the midst of industrial plenty is seen solely as an outcome of the system of production, to be solved by redistributive legislation and state control.

This book presents the complementary view. The poor are our kith and kin. Not all our relatives are likely to be among the well-to-do. If we do not know how the poor live, it can only be that we have selected against them in the constituting of our consumption rituals, and have declined invitations to join their celebrations. A rigorous sociology of the family would focus the vague criticisms from anthropology and bring them to bear upon the theory of consumption.

NOTES

Chapter 1

1. Boltanski, Luc. "Taxinomies populaires, taxinomies savantes: les objets de consommation et leur classement." *Revue Francaise de Sociologie* 11:33–34, 1970.

2. Kincaid, J. C. *Poverty and Equality in Britain: A Study of Social Security and Taxation.* Harmondsworth, England: Penguin Books, 1973.

3. National Board for Prices and Incomes. *General Problems of Low Pay* (Report no. 169). HMSO, 1971.

4. Evans-Pritchard, E. E. *The Nuer: The Political Institutions of a Nilotic People,* p. 88. Oxford: Clarendon Press, 1940.

5. Abel-Smith, B., and Townsend, P. *The Poor and the Poorest,* pp. 9–12, 57–67. London: Bell, 1965.

6. Hirschmann, Albert O. "The Changing Tolerance for Income Inequality in the Course of Economic Development." *The Quarterly Journal of Economics* 87:504–566, 1973.

7. Douglas, Mary, *Witchcraft Accusations and Confessions,* A.S.A. (Association of Social Anthropologists) Monograph no. 9. London: Tavistock, 1970.

8. Titmuss, R. M. *Commitment to Welfare,* p. 68. London: Allen & Unwin, 1968.

9. Lancaster, Kelvin. "A New Approach to Consumer Theory." *Journal of Political Economy* 74:132–157, 1966.

10. Leontieff, W. "The Internal Structure of Functional Relationships." *Econometrica* 15:361–373, 1947.

11. Michael, R. T., and Becker, G. "On the New Theory of Consumer Behaviour." *Swedish Journal of Economics* 75(4):378–396, 1973.

12. Haavelmo, T. "A Study of the Theory Of Economic Evolution." In *Contributions to Economic Analysis,* pp. 6–7. Elsevier-North Holland Publishing Co., 1964.

13. Mishan, E. J. "A Survey of Welfare Economics, 1939–59." In *Surveys of Economic Theory,* vol. 1, edited by E. A. Robinson, pp. 154–222. New York: St. Martin's Press, 1968.

14. Kuznets, Simon. *Economic Growth of Nations: Total Output and Production Structure,* pp. 75–78. Cambridge, Mass.: Harvard University Press, 1971.

15. Keynes, J. M. *The General Theory of Employment, Interest and Money,* p. 104. London: Macmillan, 1942 (first published 1936).

16. Knight, Frank. "The Ethics of Competition." *The Quarterly Journal of Economics* 37:579–624, 1923.

17. Jevons, W. S. *The Theory of Political Economy,* p. 47. London: Macmillan, 1870.

18. Bentham, Jeremy. *Principles of Morals and Legislation.* Oxford: Clarendon Press, 1789.

19. Sraffa, Piero. *Production of Commodities by Means of Commodities; Prelude to a Critique of Economic Theory.* Cambridge: Cambridge University Press, 1972.
20. Sraffa. *Production of Commodities,* p. 93.
21. Sraffa. *Production of Commodities,* p. v.

Chapter 2

1. Keynes, J. M. *The General Theory of Employment, Interest and Money,* p. 96. London: Macmillan, 1942.
2. Hart, Albert G. "Postwar Effects to Be Expected from Wartime Liquid Accumulations." *American Economic Review,* Proc. 35:345–346, 1945.
3. Fisher, Irving. *The Nature of Capital and Income.* New York, 1906; Miller, S. M.; Reissman, F.; and Seagull, A. A. "Poverty and Self-Indulgence: A Critique of the Non-deferred Gratification Pattern." In *Poverty in America,* L. A. Forman, J. L. Kornbluth, and A. Haber, eds. Ann Arbor, Mich.: University of Michigan Press, 1965.
4. Lewis, Oscar. *La Vida: A Puerto Rican Family in the Culture of Poverty.* New York: Random House, 1966; "The Culture of Poverty." *Scientific American,* October 1966, p. 25.
5. Weber, Max. *The Rise of the Protestant Ethic and the Spirit of Capitalism.* New York: Charles Scribner's Sons, 1958.
6. Weber. *The Rise of the Protestant Ethic,* p. 76.
7. Sahlins, Marshall. *Stone Age Economics,* chaps. 2 and 3. London: Tavistock, 1974.
8. Wolf, Eric R. "Types of Latin American Peasantry." *American Anthropologist* 57, 1955.
9. Boutruche, Robert. *La Crise d'une Société: Seigneurs et paysans du Bordelais pendant la Guerre de Cent Ans.* Paris: Belles Lettres, 1963 (Publications de la Faculte des Lettres de l'Universite de Strasbourg).
10. Boutruche. *La Crise d'une Société,* pp. 233–234.
11. Boutruche. *La Crise d'une Société,* pp. 566–569.
12. Fortes, Meyer. "The Structure of Unilineal Descent Groups." *American Anthropologist* 55:17–41, 1953; Smith, M. G. "On Segmentary Lineage Systems." *Journal of the Royal Anthropological Institute* 86 (part 2):39–80, 1956.
13. Dennis, N.; Henriques, F.; and Slaughter, C. *Coal Is Our Life.* London: Tavistock, 1969.
14. Bernstein, B. *Class, Codes and Control,* Vol. 1, *Theoretical Studies Towards a Sociology of Language,* chap. 11. London: Routledge & Kegan Paul, 1971; Douglas, Mary. *Cultural Bias.* Royal Anthropological Institute, Occasional Paper no. 35, 1978.
15. Peristiany, J. G., ed. *Honour and Shame, The Values of Mediterranean Society.* London: Weidenfeld & Nicolson, 1965.

16. Snyder, S. "The Quest for the Sacred in Northern Puget Sound: An Interpretation of Potlatch." *Ethnology* 14(2):149–162, 1975.

17. Campbell, John. *Honour, Family and Patronage.* Oxford: Oxford University Press, 1964; Bourdieu, Pierre. *The Sentiment of Honour in Kabyle Society.* In Peristiany, *Honour and Shame,* pp. 191–242.

18. Duesenberry, J. S. *Income, Saving and the Theory of Consumer Behavior.* Cambridge, Mass.: Harvard University Press, 1949.

19. Duesenberry. *Income, Saving and the Theory of Consumer Behavior,* p. 29.

20. Dubois, Cora. *People of Alor.*: University of Minnesota Press, Minneapolis, Minn. 1944.

21. Friedman, Milton. *A Theory of the Consumption Function.* Princeton, N.J.: Princeton University Press, 1957.

22. Friedman. *A Theory of the Consumption Function,* p. 10.

23: Bodkin, Ronald. "Windfall Income and Consumption," p. 175; Duesenberry, J. S. "Comments on Bodkin," pp. 188–191; Friedman, M. "Comments on Bodkin," pp. 191–206. Bodkin, R. "Rejoinder to Friedman," pp. 206–207. In *Study of Consumer Expenditure, Incomes and Savings,* part 4, *General Savings Relations, Permanent Income and Other Theories* (Proceedings of the Conference on Consumption and Saving, Vol. 2), edited by I. Friend and K. Jones. Philadelphia: Wharton School of Finance, 1960.

24. Brown, A., and Deaton, A. "Surveys in Applied Economics: Models of Consumer Behaviour." *The Economic Journal,* pp. 1145–1236, 1972.

25. Reid, Margaret. *Economics of Household Production.* New York, 1934.

26. Brady, D., and Friedman, R. D. *Savings and the Income Distribution,* Vol. 10, pp. 247ff. New York: National Bureau of Economic Research, 1947.

27. Friedman, M., and Kuznets, Simon. *Income from Independent Professional Practice.* New York: National Bureau of Economic Research, 1945.

Chapter 3

1. Evans-Pritchard. "The Nuer." In *The Political Institutions of a Nilotic People,* pp. 17–19. Oxford: Clarendon Press, 1940.

2. Durkheim, E. *The Rules of Sociological Method,* edited by E. G. Catlin. Chicago: University of Chicago Press, 1950.

3. Lévi-Strauss, C. *Totemism.* London: Merlin Press, 1962; *The Savage Mind.* London: Weidenfield & Nicolson, 1966.

4. Douglas, Mary. *Purity and Danger: An Analysis of Concepts of Pollution and Taboo.* London: Routledge & Kegan Paul, 1966.

5. Blau, Peter. *Exchange and Power in Social Life.* New York: John Wiley, 1964.

6. Dumont, Louis. "The Modern Concept of the Individual: Notes on Its Genesis and That of Concomitant Institutions." *Contributions to Indian Sociology* 8:13–61, 1965.

7. Berger, P., and Luckmann, T. *The Social Construction of Reality: A Treatise in the Sociology of Knowledge*. Garden City, N.Y.: Doubleday, 1966.

8. Lévi-Strauss, C. *Anthropologie Structurale*. Paris: 1958. (English translation: *Structural Anthropology*. London: Allen Lane, 1968.)

9. Cicourel, A. *Cognitive Sociology*. Harmondsworth, England: Penguin Books, 1973.

10. Snyder, Sally. "Quest for the Sacred in Northern Puget Sound: An Interpretation of Potlatch." *Ethnology* 14(2):154–156.

Chapter 4

1. Hicks, John. *A Revision of Demand Theory*, p. 166. Oxford: Oxford University Press, 1965.

2. Galbraith, J. K. *The Affluent Society*, p. 123. London: Hamish Hamilton, 1958; *Economics and the Public Purpose*, pp. 55–63. London: Andre Deutsch, 1974.

3. Barthes, Roland. *Brillat-Savarin*, pp. 7, 8, 1975.

4. Ibid, p. 12.

5. Ibid, pp. 13, 14.

6. Schutz, Alfred. *Collected Papers. 1: The Problem of Social Reality*, pp. 3–47. The Hague: Nijhoff, 1971.

7. Trollope, A. *The Prime Minister*, chap. 1. Oxford: Oxford University Press (World Classics), 1876.

8. Royal Academy Trustees. *Turner, 1775–1851*, published for the 1974–1975 exhibition.

9. Knowles, David. *The Religious Orders in England*. Cambridge: Cambridge University Press, 1948.

10. Tarde, Gabriel. *On Communication and Social Influence—Selected Papers, 1899*. Edited and introduced by T. W. Clarke. Chicago: University of Chicago Press, 1900.

11. Trollope, A. *The Eustace Diamonds*, chap. 32. Oxford: Oxford University Press (Worlds Classics), 1873.

12. Trollope. *The Eustace Diamonds*, p. 323.

13. Trollope, A. *The Prime Minister*, p. 99. Oxford: Oxford University Press (Worlds Classics), 1876.

14. Trollope. *The Prime Minister*, p. 89.

15. Kuper, Adam. "Preferential Marriage and Polygamy among the Tswana." In *Essays in African Social Anthropology*, edited by M. Fortes and S. Patterson, pp. 121–134. New York: Academic Press, 1975.

16. Glass, David V., *Social Mobility in Britain*, pp. 327–328. London: Routledge & Kegan Paul, 1966 (first published 1954).

Notes

17. Lévi-Strauss, C. *The Savage Mind*. Chicago: University of Chicago Press, 1966.

18. Douglas, Mary. "Deciphering a Meal." *Daedalus,* Winter 1972, chap. 17.

19. Tambiah, S. J. "Animals Are Good to Think, and Good to Prohibit." *Ethnology* 8(4):423–459, 1969.

20. Douglas, Mary. "Self-Evidence," Henry Myers Lecture, *Proceedings of the Royal Anthropological Institute,* 1972; reprinted in *Implicit Meanings,* by Mary Douglas. London: Routledge & Kegan Paul, 1975.

21. Memorandum submitted by the Supplementary Benefits Commission to the Royal Commission on the Distribution of Income and Wealth, May 1977.

22. Young, Michael, and Willmott, Peter. *The Symmetrical Family; A Study of Work and Leisure in the London Region.* London: Routledge & Kegan Paul, 1973.

23. Rowntree, B. Seebohm. *Poverty: A Study of Town Life,* p. 86. London: Macmillan, 1901.

24. Wildavsky, Aaron. *A Comparative Theory of Budgetary Processes,* pp. 138–139. Boston: Little, Brown, 1975.

25. Wildavsky. *A Comparative Theory,* pp. 139–165.

26. Nankivell, Owen. *All Good Gifts: A Christian View of the Affluent Society,* p. 42. London: Epworth Press, 1978.

27. Bourdieu, Pierre. "Avenir de classe et causalité du probable." *Revue Française de Sociologie* 15:3–42, 1974.

Chapter 5

1. Muth, Richard F. "Household Production and Consumer Demand Functions." *Econometrica* 34(3):699–708, 1966.

2. Houthakker, H. S. "The Influence of Prices and Incomes on Household Expenditures." *Bulletin of International Institute of Statistics* 37, 1960.

3. Van Praag, B. S. *Individual Welfare and Consumer Behaviour: A Theory of Rationality,* pp. 129, 211–213. New York: Elsevier-North Holland Publishing Co., 1968.

4. Pyatt, F. Graham. *Priority Patterns and the Demand for Household Durable Goods.* Cambridge: Cambridge University Press, 1966.

5. Lancaster, Kelvin. *Consumer Demand: A New Approach.* New York: Columbia University Press, 1971.

6. Strotz, "The Empirical Implications of a Utility Tree." *Econometricia* 25:269–280, 1957; "The Utility Tree—A Correction and Further Appraisal." *Econometrica* 27:482–488, 1959; Gorman, W. M. "Separable Utility and Aggregation." *Econometrica* 27:469–481, 1959.

7. Bain, A. D. *The Growth of Television Ownership in the United Kingdom Since the War: A Log-normal Model,* pp. 68ff. Cambridge: Cambridge University Press, 1964.

8. Prest, A. R. "Some Experiments in Demand Analysis." *Review of Economics and Statistics* 13:33–49, 1949.

9. Farrell, M. J. "Irreversible Demand Functions." *Econometrica* 20: 171–186, 1952.

10. Ironmonger, D. S. *New Commodities and Consumer Behaviour*, pp. 73–78, 100, 121–126. Cambridge: Cambridge University Press, 1972.

11. Gulliver, P. H. *The Family Herds, a Study of Two Pastoral Tribes in East Africa: The Jie and the Turkana*, pp. 38–39. London: Routledge & Kegan Paul, 1955.

12. Douglas, Mary. *The Lele of the Kasai*. Oxford: Oxford University Press (for International African Institute), 1963.

13. Paroush, J. "The Order of Acquisition of Consumer Durables." *Econometrica* 33:225–235, 1965.

14. Paroush, J. "Efficient Purchasing and Order Relations in Consumption." *Kyklos* 26:91, 1963.

15. Pyatt. *Priority Patterns*, p. 88.

16. Pyatt. *Priority Patterns*, p. 77.

17. Chamberlin, E. R. *The Awakening Giant: Britain in the Industrial Revolution*. London: Batsford, 1976.

18. Cramer, J. S. "Ownership Elasticities of Consumer Durables." *Review of Economic Studies*, pp. 87–96, 1958.

19. Lancaster, Kelvin, J. "A New Approach to Consumer Theory." *Journal of Political Economy* 174:132–157, 1966.

20. Lancaster, Kelvin, J. *Consumer Demand: A New Approach*, pp. 4–5. New York: Columbia University Press, 1971.

Chapter 6

1. Fortes, Meyer. *The Dynamics of Clanship Amongst the Tallensi*. Oxford: Oxford University Press, 1945; *The Web of Kinship Amongst the Tallensi*. Oxford: Oxford University Press, 1949.

2. Douglas, Mary, and Nicod, Michael. "Taking the Biscuit: The Structure of British Meals." *New Society*, December 19, 1974, pp. 744–747.

3. Myint, H. C. *Theories of Welfare Economics*, chap. 11. London: Frank Cass, 1948.

4. Becker, Gary. *Human Capital*. New York, 1948.

5. Granger, C. W. J. "Investigating Causal Relations by Econometric Models and Cross-spectral Methods." *Econometrica* 37:424–438, 1969; Nerlove, Marc. "Spectral Analysis of Seasonal Adjustment Procedures." *Econometrica* 32:241–286, 1964.

6. Hicks, J. "Liquidity." *Economic Journal*, pp. 787–802, 1962.

7. "The Pub and the People," *Mass Observation*, quoted in *Food Connexions* by Richard Mabey, Penguin Education, p. 47. 1970.

8. Schmöelders, G., and Biervert, B. "Level of Aspiration and Con-

sumption Standard: Some General Findings." In *Human Behaviour in Economic Affairs,* edited by B. Strumpel, pp. 213–222, 1972.

9. Veblen, T. *Theory of the Leisure Class,* 1899.

10. Leibenstein. "Bandwagon, Snob and Veblen Effects in the Theory of consumer demand." *Quarterly Journal of Economics,* pp. 183–207, 1950; *GPO Research* 3/73, p. 53, 1973.

11. Simon, Herbert A. "Decision-making in Economics." In *Resource Allocation* (Surveys of Economic Theory, Vol. 3), pp. 1–28. New York: St. Martin's Press, 1966.

Chapter 7

1. Hoyt, Elizabeth E. *Primitive Trade: Its Psychology and Economics.* London: Kegan Paul, Trench Trubner, 1926.

2. Firth, Raymond, ed. *Themes in Economic Anthropology* (A.S.A. Monograph no. 6), pp. 18–20. London: Tavistock, 1967; Barth, Fredrik. "Economic Spheres in Darfur," in *Themes in Economic Anthropology,* edited by Firth, pp. 149–173.

3. Sahlins, M. *Stone-Age Economics,* pp. 299–301. London: Tavistock, 1974.

4. Kroeber, A. L. *Handbook of the Indians of California* (Bulletin 78). Washington, D.C.: Smithsonian, Bureau of American Ethnology, 1925.

5. Kroeber. *Handbook of the Indians of California,* p. 4.

6. Dubois, Cora. "The Wealth Concept as an Integrative Factor in Tolowa-Tututni Culture." In *Essays in Anthropology Presented to A. L. Kroeber,* pp. 49–65. University of California Press, 1936.

7. Mayer, Thomas. "Investment in Human Capital and Personal Income Distribution." *Journal of Political Economy* 66:283, 1958.

8. Bohannan, P. "Some Principles of Exchange and Investment Among the Tiv." *American Anthropologist* 57:60–70, 1955.

9. Bohannan, Paul, and Bohannan, Laura. *Tiv Economy.* Northwestern University Press, Evanston, Ill.: 1968.

10. Douglas, Mary. *The Lele of the Kasai.* Oxford: Oxford University Press, 1963.

11. Douglas, Mary. "Raffia Cloth Distribution in the Lele Economy." *Africa* 28:109–122, 1958.

12. Cohen, Abner. *Custom and Politics in Urban Africa: A Study of Hausa Migrants in Yoruba Towns,* pp. 59, 66–68. University of California Press, Berkeley, Ca: 1969.

13. Cohen, *Custom and Politics in Urban Africa,* pp. 67–68.

14. Leymore, V. *Hidden Myth: Structure and Symbolism in Advertising,* pp. 125–127. London: Heinemann, 1975.

15. Malinowski, B. *The Argonauts of the Western Pacific.* London: Routledge and Kegan Paul, 1922.

Chapter 8

1. Reid Margaret, G. *Economics of Household Production.* New York: John Wiley, 1934; Becker, G. S. *Human Capital: A Theoretical and Empirical Analysis with Special Reference to Education.* New York, 1954; Nerlove, Marc. "Household and Economy: Towards a New Theory of Population and Economic Growth." *Journal of Political Economy* 82, 1974; Nerlove, Marc, and Schultz, T. W. "Love and Life Between the Censuses: Mode of Family Decision Making in Puerto Rico, 1950–1960." Rand Corporation, RM 6322 Aid, 1970; Schultz, T. W. "The Value of Children: An Economic Perspective." *Journal of Political Economy* 81(1):2–13, 1973.

2. Becker, G. S. "A Theory of Human Marriage." *Journal of Political Economy* 81(4):813, 1973; Michael, R. T., and Becker, Gary. "On the New Theory of Consumer Behaviour." *Swedish Journal of Economics* 75(4):378–396, 1973.

3. Muellbauer, John. "Household Composition, Engel Curves and Welfare Comparisons Between households: A Duality Approach." *European Economic Review* 5:103–122, 1974.

4. Schultz, T. W. *The Economic Value of Education*, pp. 66*ff.* New York: Columbia University Press, 1963.

5. Vernon, R., ed. *The Technology Factor in International Trade.* National Bureau of Economic Research, 1970.

6. Linder, Staffen B. *Essay in Trade and Transformation.* New York: John Wiley, 1961.

7. Sahlins, Marshall D. "On the Sociology of Primitive Exchange." In *The Relevance of Models for Social Anthropology*, edited by M. Banton, (A.S.A. Monograph no. 1), pp. 139–236. London: Tavistock, 1965.

8. From the *International Standard Industrial Classification of Economic Activities.* New York: Statistical Office of the United Nations; cited in *The Service Industries*, by Yves Sabolo, pp. 12, 21, 22. Geneva: ILO, 1975).

9. Sabolo, *The Service Industries*, pp. 12, 21, 22.

10. Abrams, Mark. *The Condition of the British People, 1911–1945.* London: Gollancz, 1946.

11. Department of Employment, *New Earnings Survey, 1975.* HMSO, 1976.

12. National Board of Prices and Incomes. *General Problems of Low Pay.* (Report no. 169), p. 7. HMSO, 1971.

13. Abel-Smith, B., and Townsend, Peter. *The Poor and the Poorest.* London: Bell, 1965.

14. Bowles, Samuel. "Understanding Unequal Economic Opportunity." *American Economic Review*, May 1972, p. 346.

15. Watts, Harold W. "An Economic Definition of Poverty." In *On Understanding Poverty, 1968–69*, edited by D. P. Moynihan, Chap. 2. New York: Basic Books, 1969.

16. Coates, W.; Silburn, R.; and Juster, F. Thomas. *Household Capital Formation and Financing, 1897–1962*, p. 88.

Notes

17. Moynihan, D. P. "Maximum Feasible Misunderstanding." In *On Understanding Poverty, 1968–69,* edited by Moynihan.

18. Atkinson, A. B. *Unequal Shares,* p. 19. London: Allen Lane, 1972.

19. Kuznets, Simon. *Six Lectures on Economic Growth,* pp. 58–59. London: Frank Cass, 1966.

20. Kuznets, Simon. *Population, Capital and Economic Growth: Selected Essays,* p. 293. London: Heinemann, 1973.

21. Young, Michael, and Wilmott, Peter. *Family and Kinship in East London.* London: Tavistock, 1956.

22. Bott, Elizabeth. *Family and Social Network.* London: Tavistock, 1957.

23. Hirschman, A. O. *The Strategy of Economic Development.* New Haven, Conn.: Yale University Press, 1958; Laumos, P. S. "Key Sectors in Some Undeveloped Countries." *Kyklos* 28(1):62–79, 1975.

24. Thoburn, J. T. "Exports and the Malaysian Engineering Industry: A Case Study of Backward Linkage." *Oxford Bulletin of Economics and Statistics* 35(2): 1972.

25. Hope, K. "Marriage Markets in the Stratification System." In *The Analysis of Social Mobility, Methods and Approaches,* edited by K. Hope. Oxford: Clarendon Press, 1972.

26. Coleman, D. A. "Marriage Movement in British Cities." In *Genetic Variation in Britain,* edited by D. K. Roberts and E. Sunderland. London: Taylor & Francis, 1973.

27. Coleman, D. A. "Assortative Mating in Britain." In *Equalities and Inequalities in Family Life,* edited by R. Chester and J. Peel. Academic Press, 1977.

28. Goldthorpe, John, and Lockwood, David. *The Affluent Worker in the Class Structure,* p. 124. Cambridge: Cambridge University Press, 1971.

29. Goldthorpe and Lockwood. *The Affluent Worker,* p. 104.

30. Goldthorpe and Lockwood. *The Affluent Worker,* p. 39.

31. Dennis, N.; Henriques, F.; and Slaughter, C. *Coal Is Our Life.* London: Tavistock, 1969.

32. Dennis, Henriques, and Slaughter. *Coal Is Our Life,* pp. 36, 174, 176, 191.

33. Dennis, Henriques, and Slaughter. *Coal Is Our Life,* p. 134.

34. Dennis, Henriques, and Slaughter. *Coal Is Our Life,* p. 153n.

35. Dennis, Henriques, and Slaughter. *Coal Is Our Life,* p. 225.

36. Frankenberg, Ronald. "In the Production of Their Lives, Men(?). . . . Sex and Gender in British Community Studies." In *Sexual Divisions and Society,* edited by D. L. Barker and Sheila Allen. London: Tavistock, 1976.

37. Phelps, et al. *Employment and Inflation Theory, Micro-economic Foundations,* New York: W. W. Norton, 1970.

38. Stigler, George J. "Information in the Labour Market." *Journal of Political Economy* (Supplement 5.2); 94–105, 1962.

39. Barnes, John. "Class and Committees in a Norwegian Island Parish." *Human Relations* 7:39–58, 1954.

40. Wilson, David F. *Dockers: The Impact of Industrial Change.* Fontana, 1972.

41. Plumb, J. H. *Sir Robert Walpole, the Making of a Statesman,* Vol. 1, p. 115. London: Cresset Press, 1956.

42. Bohannan, Laura. "A Genealogical Charter." *Africa,* 22(4):301–315, 1952.

Chapter 9

1. Hope, Keith, and Gouldthorpe, John. *The Social Grading of Occupations: A New Approach and Scale.* Oxford: Oxford University Press, 1974.
2. Sabolo, Yves. *The Service Industries.* Geneva: ILO, 1975.
3. Linder, Staffen B. *Essay on Trade and Transformation.* New York: Wiley, 1961.
4. Department of Employment. *Family Expenditure Survey, 1973.* HMSO, 1974.
5. Stenning, Derek. *Savannah Nomads.* Oxford: Oxford University Press, 1959.
6. Smith, David. *Industrial Britain, the North West,* p. 30. Devon: David & Charles, 1969.
7. Reid, Margaret. "Comments on Maisel and Winnick on Housing." In *Study of Consumer Expenditure, Incomes and Savings,* p. 50. Proceedings of Conference on Consumption and Saving, Vol. 1, edited by I. Friend and R. Jones. Wharton School of Finance and Commerce, Philadelphia: University of Pennsylvania, 1973.
8. Marshall, Alfred. *Principles of Economics,* Book 3, chap. 2. London: Macmillan, 1890.
9. Jevons, W. S. *The Theory of Political Economy,* p. 45. London: Macmillan, 1879.
10. Marshall, *Principles of Economics.*
11. Unpublished GPO Research, 1973.

Chapter 10

1. Rezsöhazy, Rudolph. *The Use of Time: Daily Activities of Urban and Suburban Populations in Twelve Countries,* edited by *Alexander Szalai,* pp. 449–460. The Hague: Mouton, 1972.
2. Linder, Staffen B. *The Harried Leisure Class.* New York: Columbia University Press, 1970.
3. Hirschman, Albert O. "An Alternative Explanation of Contemporary Harriedness." *The Quarterly Journal of Economics* 87:634–637, 1973.

Notes

4. Tomkins, Calvin. *Ahead of the Game*. London: Penguin, 1962.

5. Douglas, Mary. *Cultural Bias*. London: Royal Anthropological Institute, 1978.

6. Simon, H. A., and Ando, A. "Aggregation of Variables in Dynamic Systems." *Econometrica* 29(2):111–128, 1961.

7. Atkinson, A. B. *Unequal Shares: Wealth in Britain* (rev. ed.). Harmondsworth, England: Penguin Books, 1972.

8. Rosenberg, Nathan. Chapter 8 in *The Technology Factor in International Trade*, edited by R. Vernon. London: National Bureau of Economic Research, 1970.

INDEX

Index

Choice: anthropological definition of consumption and, 56, 57; demand theory in analysis of, 20–21; economic rationality and, 71–72; metaphysical judgments in, 73–74; naming in, 76; properties of goods themselves in, 110–111

Class: admission to top class in, 180–183; age and new technology in household and, 125–126; consumption patterns in definition of, 177; experience of time and, 197; food expenditure differences related to, 97; goods as information system and, 84–89; marriage and, 164; otherworldliness and balance of power between, 32–35; potlach among Skagit Indians and, 68–70; quality of goods in periodicity of consumption and, 116; saving level comparisons for, 46; services sector admission and, 182–183; social conditions for rational behavior and, 90–94; television and telephone ownership and, 99–102; wage structure of Ashton and, 167–168, 170

Clergy, 32, 33, 35

Clerical workers, and linkage study, 187–188

Clothing: as consumption marker, 66; as factor in discrimination between events, 116

Cohen, Abner, 141, 142–143

Communication: ethnomethodology on, 64; goods needed for, 95; social life and types of, 87–88; structured system of meanings in, 95

Competition: consumption and, 84; cultural factors and, 47; individual and standards of living and, 45; rules and, 39; among Yurok Indians, 137

Conspicuous consumption: acceptance of new technology and, 126; group values on saving and, 37; Veblen's analysis of leisure class and, 4

Consumers' Purchase Study (Reid), 54

Consumption: admission to top class in, 180–183; agreement from fellow consumers in, 67–70; anthropological definition of, 56–59; as circular process, 22–23; classes of, 176–194; composite commodities in, 95–98; consumption portfolio concept for household for, 123–124; distinctive patterns of, 179–180; emulation in, 47; grouping in, 176–180; income increases related to increases in, 25, 45, 46; limitations of theory of, 19–24; linkage in, 161–165; as objective of work, 21–22; order of acquisition and, 104–110; periodicities in, 114–127; personal availability and, 110–112; production and, 143; solitary consumer in, 66–67; technology of, 95–113

Control: goods as information system and, 90–94; information in consumption and, 95

Corporations, and property, 35, 36

Craftsmen, 28, 30

Creativity: in services sector, 198; in top sphere, 148

Credit: change from luxury to necessity and, 99; control over economy and, 143–144; in rich households, 160

Culture and cultural factors: in anthropological theory, 31; cash differentiated from gift in, 58–59; competition and, 47; consumption decisions as source of, 57–58; Duesenberry's theory of savings and, 45–46, 47; goods in construction of categories of, 59–62; individualist theories of use of goods and, 63–64; kinship and marriage in sharing of, 84–89; problem of synthesis of values in, 76–79; sharing names in, 76; views of saving and, 26

Currency, shell, 132, 134

Debreu, G., 20

Decision-making, and women's work, 121

Index

Ethnography: control over economy in, 143–146; periodicity in division of labor and, 120; separate economic spheres in, 131–146
Ethnomethodology, 64
Evans-Pritchard, E. E., 60
Exports, and linkage, 162

Failure, and individual responsibility, 41
Family: bequests to Church and, 35; cattle ownership among Nuer and, 60; consumption decisions and, 57–58; consumption patterns and, 180; goods as information system and, 84–89; in grid environment, 38–39; spread of television related to size of, 101
Family Expenditure Survey, 183, 190
Farmers, and information needs, 171–172
Farm families, and savings, 54
Farrell, M. J., 103
Feudalism, 33, 34
Financial sector, 164, 181
Fisher, Irving, 26
Fishermen, 171–172
Food: class differences in expenditures on, 97; as composite commodity, 96; as factor in discrimination between events, 115–116; as medium for discriminating values, 66; top social class and, 191
Fortes, Meyer, 115
Forward linkage, 162
Franciscans, 35
Franklin, Benjamin, 42
Friars, 79–80
Friedman, Milton, 47–52, 54, 55, 167
Friedman, R. D., 54
Fulani herdsmen, 184
Furniture expenditures: consumption classes and, 189–190; new technology acceptance related to, 126

Genealogical information, 174
General Post Office, 192

Gift, as differentiated from cash, 58–59
Gillray, James, 109
Glass, David, 87
Goldthorpe, John, 165, 166
Goods: construction of categories of culture and, 59–62; individualist theories on, 62–63; as material culture, 71–74; purposes for buying, 3–4; as ritual adjuncts, 65–67; uses of, 56–70
Government: consumption provided by, 57; political need for information by, 173–174; in social structure by consumption styles, 176
Greek society, 41
Grid-group analysis, 38–40, 41–42, 43, 198
Group: in Ashton study of social linkage, 166–170; individual environment and, 40; saving and, 36–38, 43
Grouping in consumption, 176–180
Growth, and scale of operations, 104
Gustation, and choice, 73–74

Halbwachs, Maurice, 195
Hausa (Sabo) people, 141–143, 143–144, 145, 148, 151, 152
Henriques, F., 166–170
Hicks, J., 71, 124
Hirschman, Albert O., 18, 197
Hobbs, Thomas, 197
Honor, and individual responsibility, 40, 41
Households: age and new technology acceptance in, 125–126; in Ashton study, 168–169; comparisons for economic structure of, 155; consumption portfolio concept for, 123–124; division of labor in, 121; order of acquisition of durable goods by, 105–107; relationships among, in economic process, 149

Housing: as consumption marker, 66; as linkage test for consumption class, 189–190
Hoyt, Elizabeth, 131–132

Index

Labor: comparison among countries for distribution of, 155; consumption theory on, 21–22; division of, *see* Division of labor; economies of scale and, 104; information needs of, 171; services sector and training of, 197; as source of wealth and power, 150

Lancaster, Kelvin, 20, 100–101, 110–111, 123

Land, as source of wealth, 150

Landlords, 41–42

Legislation, redistributive, 157, 201

Leisure: class and, 90–91; time preference in saving and, 27; top social class and, 182

Leisure class: time and consumption and, 196; Veblen's analysis of, 4

Lele tribe: admission and exclusion in, 88; social demands of expenditures among, 105; spheres of exchange among, 140, 141

Leontieff, W., 20

Level of consumption, and periodicity, 124–127

Levi-Strauss, C., 61, 87–88

Life cycle: frequency of use of objects in, 115–116; Friedman's saving theory and, 48–49, 51; goods in differentiation of intervals in, 66; social demands for expenditures during, 105

Linder, Staffen B., 152–153, 183, 196, 198

Linkage: consumer information, 170–175; consumer social, 166–170; consumer technological, 165–166; consumption classes and tests of, 183–192; grouping by consumption style and 177–180; information linkage in, 164–165; kinds of, 163; volume of social interaction and, 163–164

Liquid constraints, 123, 124

Lockwood, David, 165, 166

Luck, and individual responsibility, 40, 41

Luxuries: admission to top class and, 181; anthropological definition of, 112; change to necessity

from, 98–99; control over economy and, 143–146; distinction between material and spiritual goods and, 72; division of labor in differentiation between necessities and, 122; Engel curve in grouping of, 97; grouping by consumption style and, 179; neutrality of, in economic theory, 97–98; periodicity in consumption and quality of, 116–119; standardization of, 145; as weapons of exclusion, 131

Magic, 61–62

Malaysia, 162

Marginal method in economics, 22, 23

Market, and consumption, 56–57

Market research, 74, 176–177

Marking services: consumption and, 74–76; consumption comparisons with, 158; consumption periodicities and, 124; frequency of use of objects and, 115–116; marriage and kinship and, 164; naming in, 75–76; order of acquisition of goods and, 104; personal availability of goods and, 111–112; quality of goods in periodicity of consumption and, 118; rituals of consumption and, 81–84; scale of consumption and scale of production and, 200

Marriage: consumption and employment and, 172–173; earning potential and, 85–86; goods as information system and, 84–89; marking services and, 164; poverty and, 204–205; restricted circulation of goods and, 142, 143; social class restriction through, 39, 95; spheres of influence in tribal society and, 138, 140, 141; among Yurok Indians, 133

Marshall, 190, 191–192

Mass Observation (periodical), 124

Materialist theory of needs, 16–18, 19

223

Index